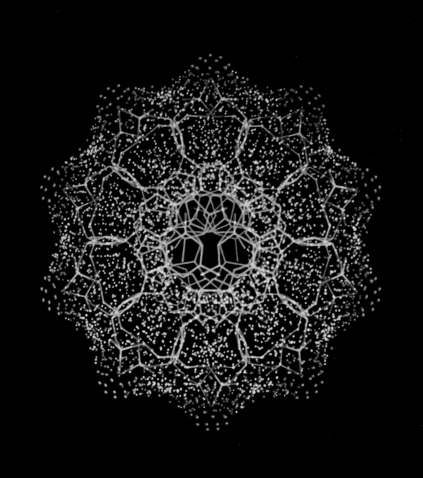

*Prepared by the Special Publications Division*
*National Geographic Society, Washington, D. C.*

ON THE BRINK OF TOMORROW:
# FRONTIERS OF SCIENCE

ON THE BRINK OF TOMORROW:
# FRONTIERS OF SCIENCE

*Contributing Authors:* DEREK deSOLLA PRICE, DONALD D. CLAYTON, BRADFORD A. SMITH, J. TUZO WILSON, RICHARD F. THOMPSON, ANTHONY CERAMI, SOLOMON H. SNYDER
*Principal Photographer:* MARK GODFREY
*Illustrator:* SUSAN SANFORD

*Published by*
THE NATIONAL GEOGRAPHIC SOCIETY
GILBERT M. GROSVENOR, *President*
MELVIN M. PAYNE, *Chairman of the Board*
OWEN R. ANDERSON, *Executive Vice President*
ROBERT L. BREEDEN, *Vice President, Publications and Educational Media*

*Prepared by*
THE SPECIAL PUBLICATIONS DIVISION
DONALD J. CRUMP, *Editor*
PHILIP B. SILCOTT, *Associate Editor*
WILLIAM L. ALLEN, WILLIAM R. GRAY, *Senior Editors*

*Staff for this Book*
MERRILL WINDSOR, *Managing Editor*
BONNIE S. LAWRENCE, *Project Editor*
SEYMOUR L. FISHBEIN, PAUL D. MARTIN, *Contributing Editors*
BONNIE S. LAWRENCE, WILLIAM L. ALLEN, *Picture Editors*
JODY BOLT, *Art Director*
H. ROBERT MORRISON, *Assistant to the Managing Editor*
MARILYN WILBUR CLEMENT, PENELOPE DIAMANTI DE WIDT, AMY GOODWIN, *Researchers;* VICTORIA I. PISCOPO, ANDY VAN DUYM, *Research Assistants*
LESLIE ALLEN, JODY BOLT, JANE H. BUXTON, CAROLYN S. HATT, KAREN M. KOSTYAL, CHRISTINE ECKSTROM LEE, JANE R. MCCAULEY, H. ROBERT MORRISON, *Picture Legend Writers*
CAROL A. ROCHELEAU, *Illustrations Assistant*

*Engraving, Printing, and Product Manufacture*
ROBERT W. MESSER, *Manager*
GEORGE V. WHITE, *Production Manager*
GREGORY STORER, *Production Project Manager*
MARK R. DUNLEVY, RICHARD A. MCCLURE, DAVID V. SHOWERS, *Assistant Production Managers;* KATHERINE H. DONOHUE, *Senior Production Assistant;* MARY A. BENNETT, *Production Assistant;* KATHERINE R. LEITCH, *Production Staff Assistant*

NANCY F. BERRY, C. REBECCA BITTLE, PAMELA A. BLACK, NETTIE BURKE, JANE H. BUXTON, MARY ELIZABETH DAVIS, CLAIRE M. DOIG, JANET A. DUSTIN, ROSAMUND GARNER, VICTORIA D. GARRETT, MARY JANE GORE, JANE R. HALPIN, NANCY J. HARVEY, SHERYL A. HOEY, JOAN HURST, ARTEMIS S. LAMPATHAKIS, VIRGINIA A. MCCOY, MARY EVELYN MCKINNEY, MERRICK P. MURDOCK, CLEO E. PETROFF, TAMMY PRESLEY, KATHLEEN T. SHEA, KATHERYN M. SLOCUM, JENNY TAKACS, CAROLE L. TYLER, *Staff Assistants*

MARTHA K. HIGHTOWER, *Indexer*

*Magnified view of a section of tissue reveals the human brain's complex circuitry. Branching out from more than ten billion nerve cells, called neurons, slender extensions— dendrites and axons—weave pathways over a total distance of about 250,000 miles. Each neuron's many dendrites receive information from other cells; its long, multiple-tipped axon transmits impulses. Through these extensions the typical neuron has the potential to communicate with several million other cells.*

PAGES 2-3: *Birthplace of stars, the Carina Nebula glows with the red light of hydrogen. Eta Carinae, the star at the nebula's center, may have a mass a hundred times that of the sun. Some astronomers predict that it will become a supernova, or brilliant exploding star—a spectacle not seen in our galaxy since 1604.*

PAGE 1: *Lacy, symmetrical fretwork of the DNA molecule suggests its intricate role in basic life processes. In this computer-generated, cross-sectional view, each dot of light indicates a single atom: blue for nitrogen, yellow for phosphorus, red for oxygen, green for carbon.*

HARDCOVER: *Like a whirling pinwheel, the spiral of our Milky Way galaxy takes shape from a computer mapping process based on radio astronomy.*

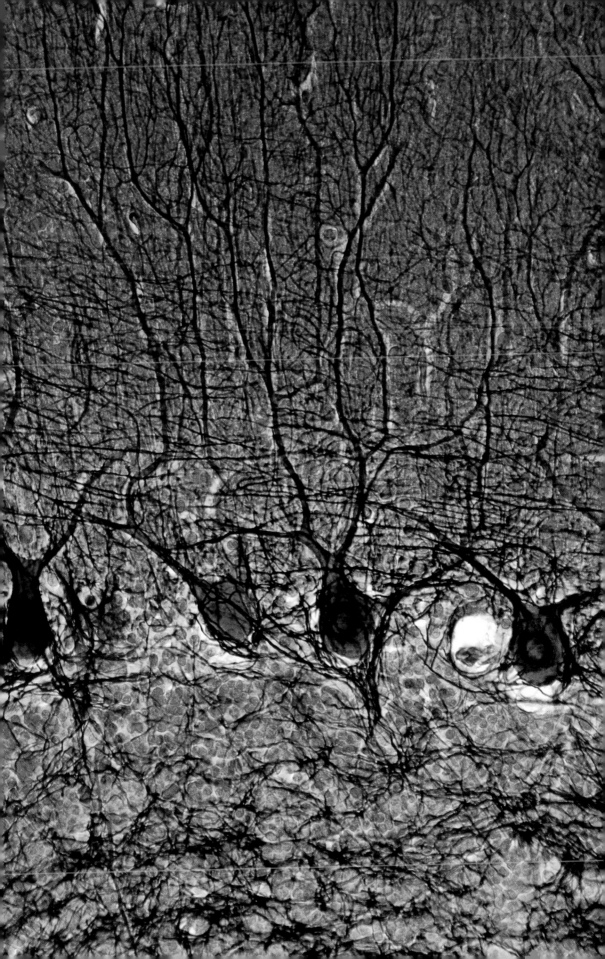

*History of the universe, scientists believe, began with a "big bang" 10 to 15 billion years ago. In time our solar system formed from condensing gas and dust, and earth's oceans emerged. In their waters, perhaps when warmed by volcanic eruptions or sparked by lightning, organic compounds formed; from them living organisms evolved. Man, one of the latest creatures to arrive, surveys the amazing ribbon of life that has unfolded from the first molecules.*

7

# SCIENTISTS AND THEIR TOOLS

*By* DEREK DESOLLA PRICE, *Ph.D.*
*Avalon Professor of the History of Science,*
*Yale University*

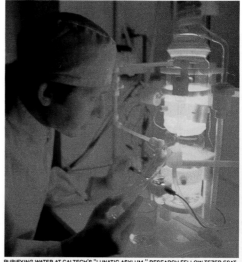

PURIFYING WATER AT CALTECH'S "LUNATIC ASYLUM," RESEARCH FELLOW TEZER ESAT PREPARES TO DATE LUNAR ROCK BY ANALYZING ITS RADIOACTIVE DECAY.

Many times in my scientific life, when inspiration has hit and I've been on the brink of a great discovery, somebody has saved me from making a fool of myself. Sometimes I have been corrected by an editor or a consultant; sometimes it is the person in the next laboratory or a colleague on the telephone; sometimes I've done it for myself. The messages vary— as direct as "That minus sign should be a plus!" or as diplomatic as "Apparently you didn't realize that Smith of M.I.T. came up with that one last year." But the effect is the same.

When I was young it was worse, because for a while I was always being upstaged by Archimedes and Euclid and a host of other pioneers of centuries ago. You have to publish your conclusions, not just to communicate or to score a point, but because you do not know if you have discovered something until your colleagues confirm that you have.

I well remember the nervousness that followed my first big piece of experimental research. I had designed a new vacuum furnace in which white-hot metals could be analyzed in infrared light, and found an effect never before observed. It was more than ten years before

UCSD GRADUATE STUDENT JEFF SCHWEITZER COLLECTS A THORNBACK RAY FOR A NEURAL-PATHWAYS STUDY.

*Around the world, in their laboratories and in the field, inquisitive scientists and skilled technicians work to advance the frontiers of human knowledge. Astronomers, physicists, geologists, biologists, and others increasingly find their areas of investigation overlapping and interlocking. Combined terms have become familiar: astrophysics, geophysics, biochemistry.*

ASTRONOMER HALTON ARP, ALMOST A LONE DISSENTER TO THE EXPANDING-UNIVERSE THEORY, STUDIES A GALACTIC IMAGE.

IN ICELAND, MEMBERS OF A GEODIMETER SURVEY TEAM MAKE LASER READINGS THAT WILL HELP DETERMINE THE RATE OF SPREAD OF THE MID-ATLANTIC RIDGE.

GENETICIST RAYMOND RODRIGUEZ DISPENSES BACTERIAL
PLASMIDS FOR RECOMBINANT DNA EXPERIMENTS.

BIOCHEMIST PAUL BERG, STANFORD UNIVERSITY'S GENE-SPLICING
PIONEER, SHARED THE 1980 NOBEL PRIZE IN CHEMISTRY.

PHYSICIST SUZANNE WILLIS REPAIRS A PARTICLE DETECTOR AT
FERMI NATIONAL ACCELERATOR LABORATORY.

IN SHARK BAY, AUSTRALIAN GEOLOGIST MALCOLM WALTER TAKES A CORE SAMPLE FROM A STROMATOLITE—A
LAYERED COMMUNITY OF MICROORGANISMS AND MUDDY SAND.

# FUSION RESEARCH: HARNESSING THE POWER OF THE STARS

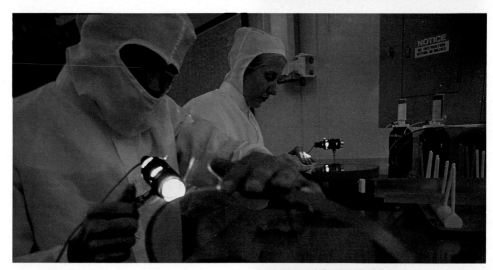

*Amid a carefully ordered jumble of test instruments (opposite), engineers adjust apparatus attached to a five-foot sphere at the Lawrence Livermore National Laboratory near San Francisco. Inside the sphere, the target chamber for the experimental laser fusion facility known as Shiva, brief bursts of a laser beam striking a tiny fuel pellet induce fusion—the conversion of lighter atoms to heavier ones, with a resulting release of energy. At top, a fuel pellet collapses, reaching temperatures greater than those at the center of the sun. Technicians cleaning and inspecting elements of the laser (above and at right) wear special head-to-toe clothing to keep the laser parts immaculate. Fusion research not only gives us greater understanding of the processes that make stars shine but in time may also help meet our energy needs.*

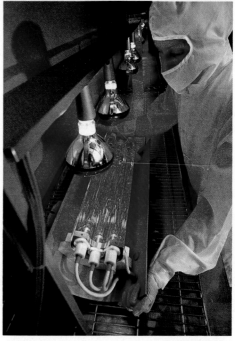

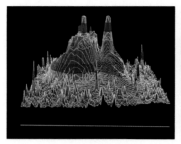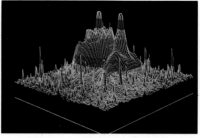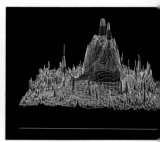

anybody else obtained the same effect—and in all that time I could only wonder if what I had found was really there!

It is rather strange that scientists feel so little freedom about their work. It's not that any director is telling them what to do; but everybody in the business acts as if there is only the one world to be discovered. However creative you are, the thing that is achieved in science seems to be already there, outside yourself and available to everyone. Personally I suppose that if the little green people came visiting in their spaceship from Sirius, everything about them might be alien, but I would still expect them to know the velocity of light and the Pythagorean theorem—not by that name, of course—because that's the way the universe is.

Perhaps this is what distinguishes science from the other grand creativities of humans. When a Beethoven or a Picasso creates, his work is uniquely a product of his personality. Boyle and Einstein had personalities, too, but in a real sense they could not create freely. The style may be theirs, but the content is dictated by the way the world is, and the way in which it is already known. There is no likelihood that Beethoven and Mozart would compose identical symphonies; but at almost the same time that Robert Boyle discovered the principle labeled Boyle's law, a French scientist, Edme Mariotte, independently defined the same law. Continental Europeans, in fact, still call it by his name.

**S**cience behaves like a giant jigsaw puzzle that is gradually being put together by all the scientists who have ever been. Each piece represents some bit of knowledge, and the various regions of the puzzle correspond to the fields of science. The living edge of the puzzle, where you can add new pieces—if you are clever enough and quick enough—is the frontier. The rule of the game is that nothing comes easily; anything that can readily be done *has* been done. You must look around for new conditions where pieces have just been laid down; only in this way can you find new pieces to add for yourself.

Thus science displays a cumulative enterprise. Each new piece of knowledge tends to give rise to opportunities for further growth, so that peninsulas extend out from each active research front. From time to time a new peninsula starts or the area between two adjacent peninsulas gets filled in quickly, producing the phenomenon of "breakthrough."

It all goes very quickly because the birthrate of scientific knowledge—the rate at which new pieces enable more to be added—is enormous. That rate for centuries has been about 7 percent a year—seven new pieces annually for each hundred pieces already fitted together. Compared with that, the human population increase is very slow, usually less than 2 percent a year.

This explosive growth of science will doubtless continue, although obviously it cannot maintain such a high rate indefinitely. There have been several interesting and important consequences of such rapid growth. Both the body of knowledge and the number of people working at the scientific frontiers have doubled every 15 to 20 years, so that there are always many more younger people and newer discoveries than older. If the average scientist's professional life covers about three such doubling periods, it follows that close to 90 percent of all the scientists who have ever lived are at work right now. If you are in your forties, half of all the world's scientific knowledge

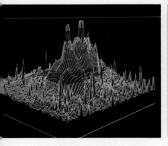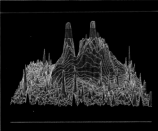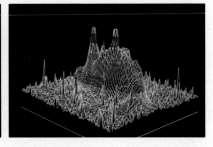

has been produced since you left school!

Each of the sciences that we pursue today had its origin in Babylonian or Greek antiquity. The structure of modern science, however, came into being through a set of fundamental changes that constitute the scientific revolution of the 17th century.

First, the invention of printing and the advent of the newspaper and other periodicals had led to the scientific journal, which permitted prompt reporting of discoveries. New information could reach far more people in much less time. Then the invention of new mathematical methods by Isaac Newton produced the first great unification of science, reconciling the calculations and terminology used in astronomy and mechanics.

The last change—and probably the most fundamental one—came about with the realization that experimenting with instruments could reveal things about the world that nobody had known before. Extending the senses with telescopes and microscopes, producing new physical conditions with vacuum pumps and electrostatic generator machines, accurately measuring things that had only been crudely gauged—like heat with the thermometer, and air pressure with the barometer—gave scholars a whole new universe to reason about.

Ever since, such instruments and their successors have been a major force in science. Quite often those who ponder the scientific enterprise concentrate on the purely intellectual side of things, and see the process as the enunciating of a succession of theories that then have to be tested by some kind of experimentation. That is the theoretician's way of looking at it. An experimentalist like myself evaluates the force of the instruments and experiments rather differently.

*Peaks and vales of a computer-drawn image reveal the complexity of the Whirlpool galaxy, also known as M 51. Today scientists tap computer technology for much more than the answers to complicated mathematical problems. In this case, an astronomer used a computer to break five telescopic photographs into 20 million individual light readings. Computer graphics transformed this mass of numbers —humanly indigestible in their raw form—into a comprehensible map of the galaxy. The two highest peaks represent the bright nuclei; the foothills correspond to dim, extended features. For a three-dimensional view, scientists can rotate the image, studying the galaxy from all angles.*

PAGES 14-15: *Six eyes of the Multiple Mirror Telescope peer at the sky from the summit of Mount Hopkins south of Tucson. A computer coupled to a television camera aligns the telescope's six mirrors, each about 72 inches in diameter, to produce a single sharp image. This revolutionary design provides the light-gathering capacity of a 176-inch conventional reflector, enabling astronomers to study very faint, distant galaxies.*

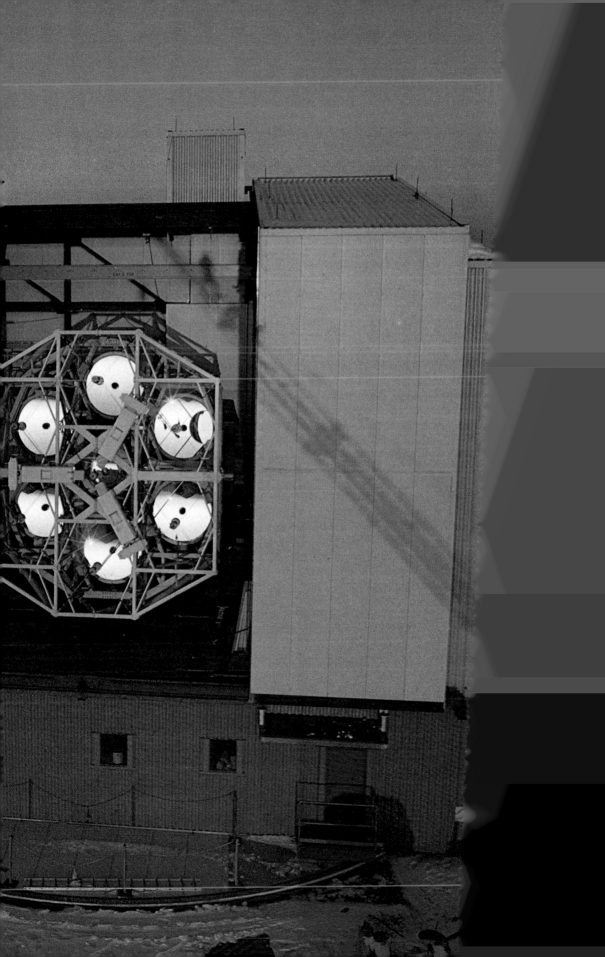

I keep seeing a cunning and wonderful craft of experimental science wrought by a bunch of people who have brains in their fingertips and think with sealing wax and string. I recall examples such as Cambridge's C.T.R. Wilson, who was a mountaineering fanatic. Intrigued by mountaintop clouds, he duplicated them in a neat laboratory apparatus. Almost by accident, the equipment proved its value in experimental uses: The famed Wilson cloud chamber was for years the best method for studying processes of radioactivity.

Certainly from time to time we set up an experiment carefully and deliberately to test some hypothesis. Much more often, and as a part of science that tends to produce spectacular and revolutionary change, we find we have some new tool or technique available and we put it through its paces to see what it will do. In 1609 the Italian mathematics professor Galileo Galilei was consulted about a military spyglass invented by the Dutch. When he tried fitting two spectacle lenses together in a lead tube, he had no idea that his crude telescope would open up to him the sight of mountains on the moon and satellites revolving around Jupiter. Similarly, we never know whether playing with a new method for making or detecting very short radio waves will reveal a new universe of invisible stars, give us radar, lead to production of microwave cookers, or arrest some types of cancer. We always have our expectations, but the most exciting frontiers of science tend to appear when some new technique reveals something that was not anticipated.

Today science is so thoroughly bound up with technology that it is difficult to disentangle the two by any simple definitions. My personal approach is to say that when you investigate nature in an area such as physics, chemistry, biology, or astronomy and you discover and record its regularities, your work is basic science. If, on the other hand, the result of your effort is some new method or machine or tangible product, it is technological research. What is most important is that such research is not simply the application of basic science, but a parallel mode of investigation.

Most of the old technologies like metalworking, pottery making, and textile weaving grew up by themselves before there was any science that could be useful to them and lend an understanding of problems and solutions. Eventually, and very gradually, there were advances. People like Josiah Wedgwood, trying out all sorts of ceramic techniques and making new kinds of porcelain and other products, learned a great deal about the nature of the materials. But it is only much later that we have progressed enough to understand why ceramics work the way they do, and to create new ones for such special purposes as the heat-shield tiles on the space shuttle *Columbia*. In general the technologies first developed independently of science, and then the new science was squeezed from them when we tried to understand what was going on. The science of thermodynamics owes much more to the steam engine than ever the steam engine owes to the application of thermodynamics.

The big change that ushered in the new age of science-based technologies came rather suddenly around 1800. A key discovery—taking us from the old low technologies that grew of themselves to the new high technologies that came out of scientific laboratories—was recognition of current electricity and the invention of the electric battery.

That discovery did not happen because anybody was looking for a new source of power or something to make light bulbs and telephones work. It came about while Luigi Galvani, a professor of anatomy at Bologna, was searching for the secret of life. He began studying the way in which the muscles in frogs' legs would twitch when they received an electric shock from an electrostatic generator—one of those special instruments that came out of the scientific revolution. Galvani noticed that the frog muscles contracted when two different metals were in contact with the frog legs at the same time.

Then the physicist Alessandro Volta realized that the frog legs were in fact irrelevant: It was the contact between the two dissimilar metals that produced the effect. He promptly constructed a device comprising many pairs of metal disks, each pair separated by a pad wetted with

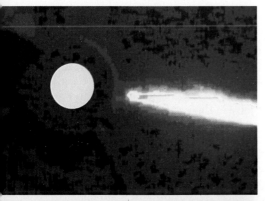

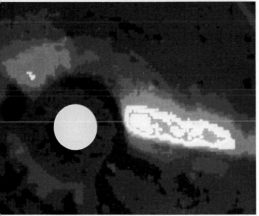

*Streaking toward its doom, a comet races through the outer solar atmosphere on a collision course with the sun (top). Hours later, a halo of debris from the vaporized comet extends millions of miles above the solar surface (bottom). Recorded by an earth-orbiting satellite in 1979, these images of an object colliding with the sun represent a first for space science. A coronagraph, designed to mask the bright solar disk for better viewing of the faint corona, detected the comet's luminous tail.*

a weak acid; this rudimentary battery yielded a continuous electric current. It was a characteristically roundabout path to new technology.

Curiously enough, the battery was initially perceived not as a power source but as a device for making chemical changes by the process of electrolysis. In the hands of people like Humphrey Davy, it led to the rapid discovery of new chemical elements. One of these gave rise to a bit of schoolboy doggerel:

> *Sir Humphrey Davy*
> *didn't like gravy,*
> *and lived in the odium*
> *of having discovered sodium.*

In less than a single generation this technique and its repercussions established the basic procedures of modern chemistry, with its beakers, coils, and Bunsen burners. When I was a child and first told my family I wanted to be a scientist, I am sure their reaction was drawn from a stereotype established during this period. A scientist was a person in a white lab coat who puttered around with test tubes and a lot of electric wiring.

Actually I worked in optics and mathematical theory, and almost never wore a lab coat. I did spend a lot of time designing apparatus. When I did experimental work, it was with spectroscopes and polarimeters, and my best skill was an ability to polish tiny metal specimens into flat mirrors without contaminating their surfaces.

For glassblowing and metalworking there were splendid old technicians who had grown up in college laboratories and workshops. A large part of my education was learning, by trying to copy them, just what they could do that I could never do myself. Thomas Edison and Ernest Rutherford had accomplished much of their work by employing to the limit manual geniuses of this sort.

The human effects of the two 19th-century sciences of electricity and chemistry were spectacular, and quite different from anything that science had done before. For the first time substances could be analyzed and synthesized. Materials could be made pure and reproducible, and no longer had to be gathered from strange and distant parts of the world where they occurred naturally.

Chemistry transformed medical pharmacy, and the understanding of chemistry deeply affected all the material technologies. Perhaps the greatest successes were in agricultural chemistry, where fertilizers were developed that made old, dead lands new; in color chemistry, where synthetic dyes breathed new life into the textile industry; and in the field of explosives with inventions such as Alfred Nobel's dynamite, which would transform both warfare and heavy construction, and yield some of its profits to establish the Nobel prizes.

Electricity in its own right became a major subject of laboratory experiment, yielding basic science on the one hand and suggesting industrial applications on the other. Among the results were the achievements of the inquisitive Edison, the coming of electric power and signaling, and the birth of an electronic age. It was this sort of development that led to our speaking of science-and-technology in a single breath.

**O**ne development in the area of electricity and magnetism was a new sort of experimentation using little modules of apparatus that could be connected, wiring together batteries and meters, resistances and coils. As scientists formulated new hypotheses, they undertook to test them in this way; and this preoccupation tended to obscure the fact that the chief burden of laboratory work was still the use of techniques to turn up new and often unexpected information.

Nevertheless this new phase of science, coming out of electricity, chemistry, and such technological advances as the steam engine, led to a series of unifying principles. They included James Clerk Maxwell's electromagnetic theory, which also gave us a basis for understanding the nature of light; and a thermodynamic theory that related heat and even acoustics to Newton's unification of mechanics and astronomy. Kingdoms may be won by dividing and conquering, but the advances of modern science have been won largely by uniting the diverse fields of investigation into a set of very general and fundamental problems.

In the early days of the modern era, when science was still called "natural philosophy," very few people were actu-

ally paid to do scientific research. For the most part such investigation was a labor of love carried out by gentlemen of means, traditionally including not only members of the professions—teachers and physicians, lawyers and clergymen—but also wealthy aristocrats who had leisure time and could afford to buy their own books and instruments.

In the big expansion of science and technology in the 19th century—with its developing fields of chemistry and electricity, the proliferation of machinery and means of transportation, the advances in surgery using antiseptics and anesthesia—there was a surge in professional education of scientists. The main mission was training people to be practicing surgeons, pharmacists, engineers, chemists, and teachers. But the professors had to keep up with the rapidly advancing front of science, and to this end they had to participate in research themselves and use their graduate students as assistants. Typically they were not paid extra for this scientific work; it was an integral part of their duties as advanced teachers at colleges and universities. In turn the educational institutions provided the instruments and laboratories, just as they had to provide libraries and other essential support facilities.

World War I involved plenty of engineering but very little science. Indeed, many of the younger scientists died on the battlefields as combat soldiers. In World War II there was a huge difference in attitude regarding the need for scientific contribution, illustrated by the sophisticated applications of radar, the development of the atomic bomb, and a much more intensive use of the whole range of science and technology.

After the war, with the organization of the National Science Foundation and

*Rocket engines ignited, the space shuttle* Columbia *begins lift-off from Kennedy Space Center on its third successful mission. Designed to ferry men and equipment into orbit, the reusable shuttle may represent a big step toward colonizing space. As a new scientific tool it holds great promise for astronomy, biomedicine, communications, and defense.*

## ACTIVE VOLCANO: A FIERY LABORATORY

*Steam and gases drift skyward from the lava dome inside the crater of Mount St. Helens in southwestern Washington. At right, the volcano's fourth explosive eruption in ten weeks—on July 22, 1980— slowly wanes. Since the end of 1980, through the use of sensitive instruments placed in the crater, geologists have predicted all of Mount St. Helens' eruptions at least five days in advance.*

numerous other governmental and private institutions, a new system of research funding was developed. Successful applicants for research grants received not only personal compensation but also payment of the expenses of the research itself and those of the institution housing the activity. Over the last three decades this approach has fundamentally altered the management of research activities, and a large part of the scientific population have come to depend on such funding rather than on teaching appointments for their bread and butter. As industrial applications of scientific and technological research increased, the research and development budgets of corporations also became major sources of financial support for scientists.

Nevertheless, in 1965 the United States reached an important milestone. For at least a century before that, the funding of science—like the numbers of people involved, and the resulting body of knowledge—had enjoyed steady and dramatic growth. The rate of increase in expenditures had been about 10 percent a year. Finally, and inevitably, some sort of saturation of the economy by science took place, and in 1965 the growth in funding came to an abrupt halt.

Since then, the money available for research and development in this country has declined, in real terms, every year. And there seems to be no reason to anticipate any change in that situation in the near future.

It must be remembered that what has been at stake is the growth rate of the funding, not the continued activity of the researchers. We still have the largest scientific establishment in history, and it is still producing huge amounts of innovation in ideas as well as in instruments and machines. The big change has been that we no longer have free growth. Today we do not support new research just because it is high in quality and attractive in its usefulness. With financial support limited in the universities, in industry, and in government agencies, some older activity has to be discontinued or wound down in order for a new one to start; and we are therefore very concerned about the process of setting priorities.

In the international setting, the position is even more complex. Although the

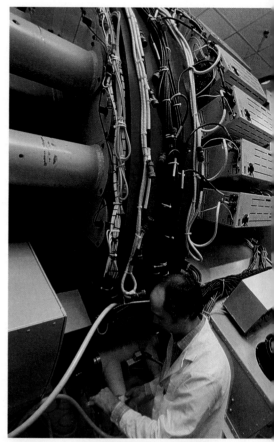

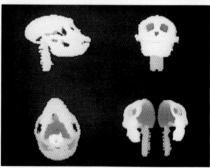

*Latest of the diagnostic imaging devices used in medical research, the DSR ("dynamic spatial reconstructor") can look into the body from any angle, isolate an organ, display its image in three dimensions, rotate it, even dissect it on the computer screen. The scan above shows the skull of a live rhesus monkey. At top, technician Sidney Whitlock of the Mayo Clinic's Biodynamics Research Unit examines some of the machine's X-ray tubes.*

most developed nations have reached ceiling conditions and have had to give up free growth, many others, some with very large populations, have actually gained speed and continue to grow rapidly. In fact, the world's total scientific effort is increasing almost as fast as it did before 1965, even though the big industrialized countries have cut back severely. Science and technology are exploding into the whole world, and are no longer a monopoly of the few largest nations.

The intellectual structure of science has now turned full circle from its earliest beginnings. Long ago in Mesopotamia, in the fertile valley where civilization took root, the Sumerians developed writing and, on clay tablets, inscribed accounts of the creation of man—who we are and where we came from. In that same valley the Babylonians, puzzling over the nature of the universe, carefully observed the sky and calculated the movements of the planets. Now that radically new machines have been devised to explore the substructure of the atom, and the space age has given astronomers new tools, our attention again is focused on the heavens and on the mystery of creation—perhaps to be explained by the cosmology of the "big bang."

In the latest phase of the history of science, experimental physicists, chemists, and biologists have brought new evidence to bear upon the mysteries of life that engaged Galvani. The clues he sought were not where he had been looking, in the power of living things to move. Rather, they lie in the genetic process that determines the form and structure of those living things—the blueprints that make individuals different versions of a single species, and that permit one species to evolve from another and then perpetuate itself.

Recently it has seemed that yet another scientific revolution is almost upon us. The impact of the computer is comparable to that of the telescope and microscope in the early days of the first scientific societies. Those instruments increased our knowledge of the world well beyond what was revealed by the unaided eye. What has happened now—from a realization of the versatility of the transistor, a discovery as accidental as that of the qualities of combination lenses—is that the capabilities of computers have increased far beyond the "number-crunching" for which they were used at first. We are beginning to get computers that can beat humans at chess. It cannot be long before even more advanced versions can be programmed to relate bits of knowledge, at least within certain categories, as well as the human brain—and then even better. In the 17th century it felt pretty spooky, I am sure, to realize that there were mountains on the moon that the unaided eye could not see. In our own time it is equally spooky to know that there are mathematical theories that can be proved by computers but not by a human brain.

I am sure that we will get used to this new clothing for the naked brain. What is even more exciting is that just as we get to this point, we are able to turn the new techniques and instruments of science to the study of the brain itself, examine its circuitry, and try to determine what makes it malfunction.

The human brain is enormously more complex than any electronic computer at present; but as we learn more about both, it is likely that computers will change radically, and be enhanced with three-dimensional memories and logics or perhaps even with the use of organic molecules instead of silicon chips.

Similarly, we have come to know much about the nature of the earth itself; and by studying other planets and their physics, we can do much more than catalog their minerals. Now we can see something of why the earth has the form and behavior it does. Indeed, we are coming very near to having a controlling knowledge of parts of our environment at the very point when we seem to be sorely endangering it with our new powers.

As I look to the future, it seems reasonable to expect all the main frontiers of science described in this book to expand prodigiously and to cross-fertilize one another. I expect astronomy, the most ancient of the sciences, to continue to be central to our efforts, spinning off benefits that we cannot begin to predict. And I expect computerized artificial intelligence to team up with the human brain to change the very pattern of thought itself.

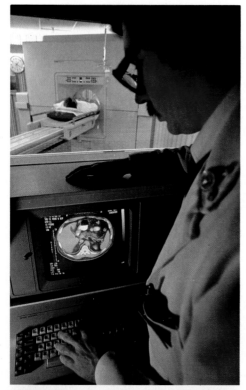

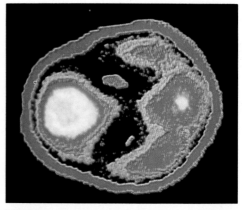

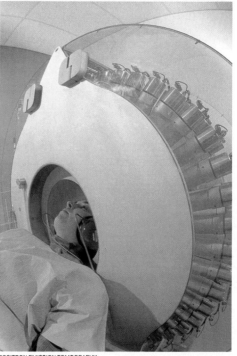

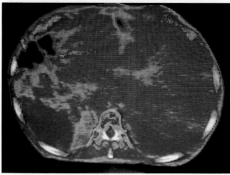

COMPUTERIZED TOMOGRAPHY

POSITRON EMISSION TOMOGRAPHY

*Most widely distributed of the external diagnostic imaging devices, the CT ("computerized tomography") scanner visualizes thin cross sections of the body. As its X-ray equipment rotates around the patient, tissues of varying densities absorb the radiation in different degrees. The resulting images appear on a television screen. Laboratory supervisor William Hosko can manipulate the image or compare it with other "slices" to find damage or tumors. The sharp image on Hosko's screen demonstrates the progress in resolution and definition since 1976, date of the abdominal scan below. CT has revolutionized diagnostic procedures.*

*A newer technique, "positron emission tomography," emphasizes function instead of structure. The PET scanner can trace blood flow through the heart, for example, or monitor the activity of the brain (top). The patient, injected with radioactive glucose, lies within a ring of gamma-ray detectors. From the rate of the sugar's assimilation by tissue, as measured by its radioactive emissions, the scanner projects an image of internal functioning on a screen; the faster the rate, the greater the degree of activity. PET scans find their most dramatic application in brain studies, and offer great promise for research into neurological illness.*

# MEDICAL IMAGING: BODY SCANS SHOW FORM OR FUNCTION

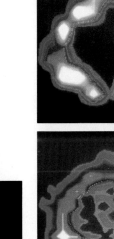

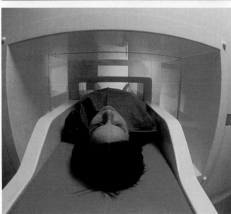

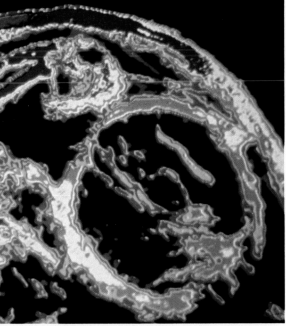

SONOGRAPHY (ULTRASOUND SCANNING)

NUCLEAR MAGNETIC RESONANCE

*Head, arm, and hand of an unborn child show up clearly on the sonogram above. Safest of the diagnostic imaging techniques, only sonography—also known as ultrasound scanning—has the approval of doctors for use in examining developing fetuses. Inaudible high-frequency sound waves, beamed into the womb in short pulses, create echoes that reflect tissue density; electronically transformed, the sounds become visual images on a screen. Used to check a baby's development and position, confirm twins or triplets, or diagnose certain abnormal conditions, sonograms make pregnancy and delivery safer for both mother and child.*

*Still experimental method of investigation and diagnosis called "nuclear magnetic resonance" can discriminate between healthy and diseased tissues. To produce an image, coiled magnets surrounding a patient align atoms of hydrogen in a magnetic field; detectors then record the atoms' reactions. Because NMR has no known harmful side effects, physicians expect to use it frequently to monitor a patient's physiological changes during treatment of such diseases as multiple sclerosis and rheumatoid arthritis. Since the first human NMR scan in 1977 (top: a normal chest) and the 1978 scan of a cancerous lung (center), the technique's imaging has greatly improved in detail.*

# 3-D VISUALIZATION OF BRAIN TUMORS

*Vivid three-dimensional views produced by computer from hundreds of two-dimensional CT scans precisely locate brain tumors and reveal their size and shape. Colors indicate varying densities of tissue: the skull, yellow; tumors, red; swelling around a tumor, blue. Below, a dense, normal membrane between the*

*left and right hemispheres separates two tumors. The images at right show a skull's exterior (top); inside the same skull, an arrowhead-shaped tumor (center); and (in a different patient) inflammation around a large tumor. With the computer's aid, surgeons can remove tumors as small as a pinhead.*

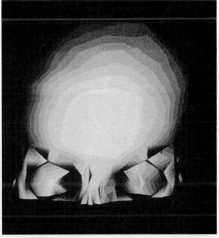

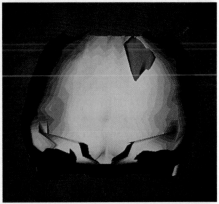

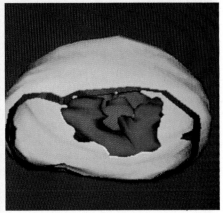

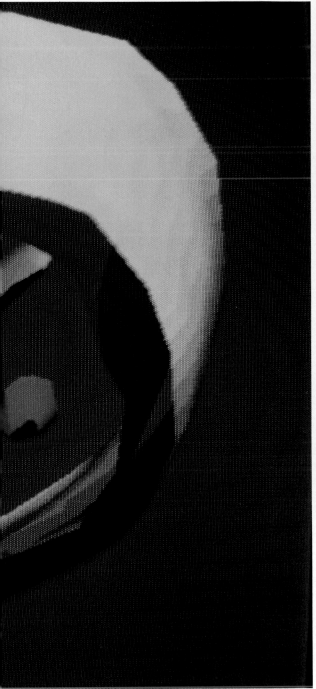

# THE UNIVERSE: QUASARS TO QUARKS

By DONALD D. CLAYTON, *Ph.D.*
*Andrew Hays Buchanan Professor of
Astrophysics,
Rice University*

*The big bang!*

Then chaos. Chaos everywhere. No galaxies, no stars, no life, not even any chemical compounds. Just radiation and bare particles. Constantly moving, violently colliding, interacting to create new particles—and to annihilate others.

Heat. Unimaginable temperatures corresponding to the energy of those chaotic particles. A brilliant bath of light and X rays.

Unbounded space. No center. No edge. Energy everywhere, in all the fundamental forms that energy may assume.

Expansion. Despite gravity, rapid expansion everywhere. Every region receding from every other—just as a rubber balloon expands without one part's ever overtaking another.

Cooling. More room for the particles. The stretching of space lowers their energies, and thus their temperatures.

Finally it is over, the chaos of particle creation and destruction. But space continues to expand, and so the intense light becomes dimmer. The remaining particles of matter, cooling and floating now, clump together into clouds of gas. Gravity collapses the clouds into galaxies, stars, planets. . . .

This is the picture presented by the

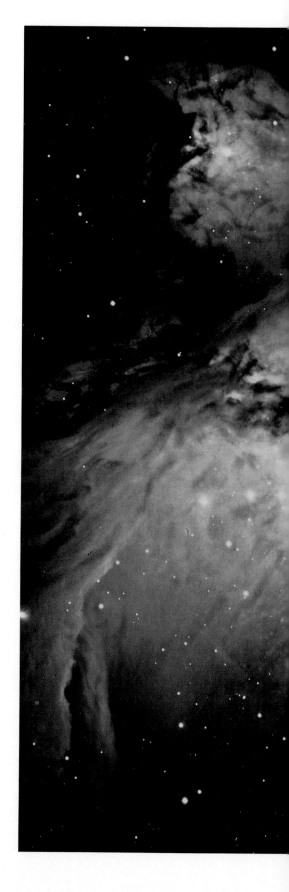

*Great Nebula in Orion glows in remarkable detail from a new color process developed by astrophotographer David Malin. Within this turbulent cosmic nursery, astronomers can study various stages in the formation of new stars.*

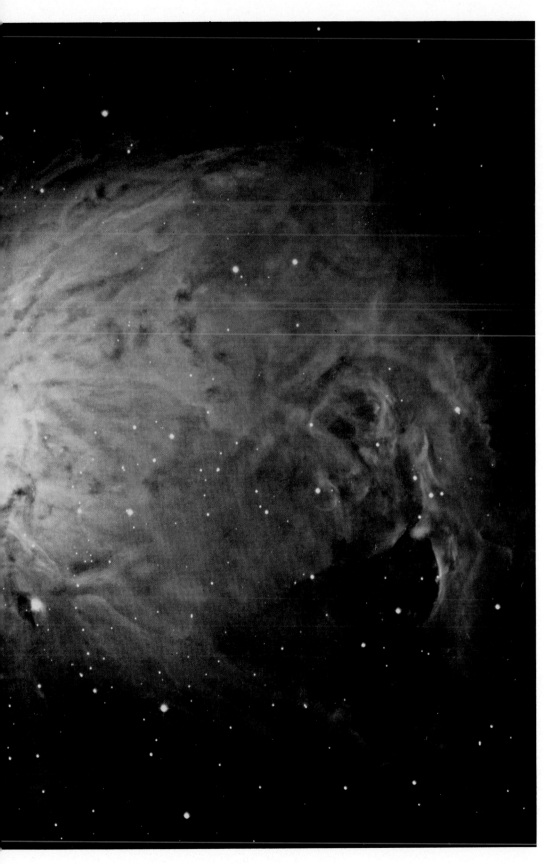

# THE TOKAMAK: FUSION BY MAGNETIC CONFINEMENT

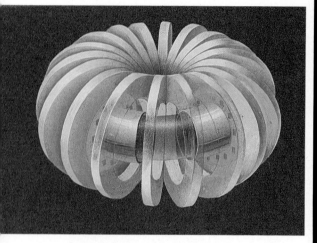

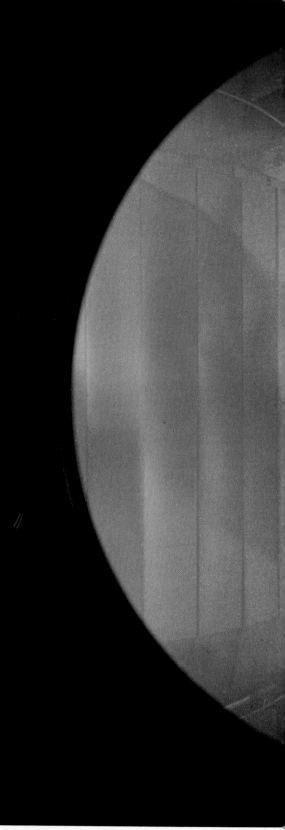

*Eerie halo surrounds superheated gas inside the fusion chamber (right) of PDX, a laboratory reactor at Princeton University in New Jersey. First developed in the Soviet Union, this type of reactor is called a "tokamak," from the Russian acronym for a doughnut-shaped magnetic chamber. In the diagram above, giant magnets ring the fusion chamber. Their magnetic fields force the gas away from the walls of the chamber; contact would cool the gas. Electric currents running through some of the windings, shown above as small rectangles in the cross section, help heat the gas to a temperature several times that of the sun's interior—so hot that the electrons of atoms separate from the nuclei. At such temperatures the gas— the denser area in the photograph at right—emits no visible light. The intense magnetic fields also squeeze the atomic nuclei of the gas closer together, greatly increasing the frequency of their collisions. The colliding nuclei fuse into new, heavier nuclei, converting (for example) hydrogen into helium and releasing huge amounts of energy.*

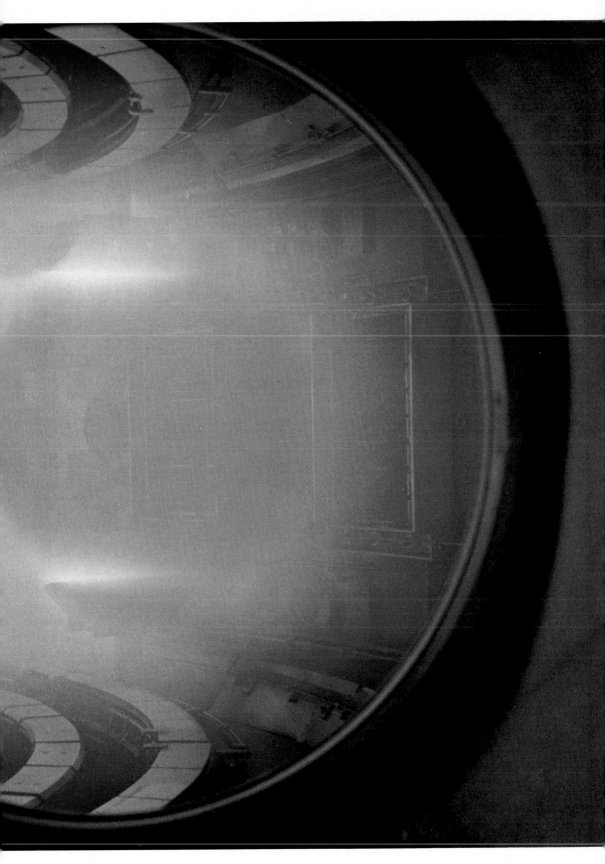

"big-bang" theory of the origin of the universe: the violent expansion of a superhot, supermassive fireball, and the chaotic aftermath. It is a scenario inferred from observations and deduced from the laws of physics. It is not absolutely certain, because we cannot be sure that all of the laws are correctly understood and the observations correctly interpreted. There is an old and wise saying: "What is science is not certain; and what is certain is not science."

When I was in graduate school in the late 1950s, there was little talk about the big bang. The expansion of the universe was a lively topic, but pushing back to the explosive beginning was a daring step. Albert Einstein himself had hesitated to take it. Instead, he modified his equations—much to his later regret—in an attempt to construct a model of the universe that did not expand. Only a couple of intrepid pioneers—the Russian mathematician Alexander Friedmann and Belgian priest-cosmologist Georges Lemaître—marked out the path that, a few decades later, most follow.

It is a staggering mental exercise to contemplate the structure of the universe, so awesomely do its scale and grandeur dwarf all human experience. We live on a small planet orbiting a typical star in the Milky Way galaxy, which itself contains two hundred billion stars. The universe is full of other galaxies, arranged in clusters. If we visualize the Milky Way as a small coin, the other galaxies in our group would be separated on average by about a foot, and the average distance between clusters of galaxies would be about 20 feet. That pattern continues in all directions as far as we can see.

In the early decades of this century the studies of astronomers Vesto Melvin Slipher, Edwin Hubble, and Milton Humason established the first evidence for an expanding universe. They showed that the other galaxies are moving away from our own. Moreover, the more distant ones recede faster.

Of course, an astronomer does not actually see the motion of the galaxies. They are much too far away for a change of position to be noticed over many human lifetimes. Their movement is measured by analyzing the light waves coming from them. The farther away the galaxy, the faster it is traveling away from us, thus the more its light waves have lengthened. As they lengthen, their pattern moves toward the red end of the spectrum. Scientists call this effect the "red shift."

The retreat of the galaxies has two immediate implications. The first is that if the expansion continues forever, the universe will become more and more sparsely occupied, until it is virtually empty and dead. That will not happen, of course, if the expansion stops and contraction begins. In this concept—sometimes called the "big crunch"—gravitational force eventually overcomes the push of expansion, and the universe collapses back to the fireball stage.

The second implication of receding galaxies pertains not to the end of the universe but to its beginning. Galaxies that are now far apart must once have been close together. About 10 to 15 billion years ago, calculations show, the galaxies would have been touching one another. Thus the average density of the entire universe would have been as great as that of an individual galaxy today. It follows that the galaxies did not then exist as separate entities.

The principle of receding galaxies is explained by a big-bang universe, but it does not *prove* a big-bang universe. For a good many years there was much discussion of an alternative theory advanced by three British scholars, Hermann Bondi, Thomas Gold, and Fred Hoyle. They developed versions of a "steady-state" theory. According to their arguments, the universe expands as in Einstein's equations, but new matter is constantly created to fill the growing voids. The steady-state universe has no beginning and no end—and, of course, no big bang. Ancient, dying galaxies coexist with young and active ones.

The carefully reasoned steady-state theory won many adherents, but today it does not find favor because it doesn't explain other phenomena as well as the big-bang theory does.

When I asked Fred Hoyle about his own evaluation of the evidence against the steady-state model, he replied with a reference to an accidental discovery at Bell Laboratories in 1965. "I had a bad

*Giant superconducting magnets glide into place in the central chamber of the Mirror Fusion Test Facility at the Lawrence Livermore National Laboratory in Livermore, California. Such units will plug both ends of the 75-foot-long cylindrical chamber, creating powerful magnetic fields to contain superheated fusion fuel.*

feeling about the 3-degree background radiation right from the beginning," said the brilliant Yorkshireman—and I understood, for that discovery greatly bolstered the concept of the big bang.

At the Bell labs, radio astronomers Arno Penzias and Robert Wilson had been listening for galactic radio waves with a large horn-shaped antenna, but were plagued by unexplained noise picked up by the antenna. By cooling their equipment with liquid helium to -452°F, or 4°Kelvin—only 4 degrees above absolute zero—they found that thermal radio waves were in fact coming from all parts of the sky, and not from heat in their own apparatus.

The discovery met other scientists' predictions that the blast of radiation released in the big bang would by now have cooled and stretched to radio wavelengths. The radiation measured by Penzias and Wilson corresponded to a source with a temperature of 3°K—clearly detectable by their very cold receiver.

Realization that the universe was full of radio waves with a temperature of only 3°K was a pivotal moment in the history of cosmology. After many subsequent measurements confirmed their astonishing breakthrough, Penzias and Wilson were awarded the Nobel Prize in Physics.

Additional confirmation of the big bang comes from observation of the chemical composition of the universe. In particular, the galaxies seem to have formed from a mixture of hydrogen and helium, the two lightest elements, in a consistent ratio of 14 to 1. This mystified astronomers until they realized that the big bang would establish such a ratio very early in its expansion.

The calculations are intricate and based on recent advances in particle physics. They indicate that, about three minutes after the big bang, the formation of hydrogen and helium nuclei began to stabilize—at a ratio of 14 to 1. This probably explains why astronomers find these elements in that same ratio throughout the universe, although some serious doubters remain.

The big bang also offers a hint of why galaxies formed at a specific stage in the expansion. For a long time, temperatures were too hot and atoms were kept moving too fast *(Continued on page 38)*

# ANTARES AND OMEGA: FUSION BY LASER BOMBARDMENT

*Window made of clear polycrystalline salt frames a staff technician at Los Alamos National Laboratory in New Mexico. Used in the Antares laser fusion device, the salt panes transmit radiation at infrared wavelengths that ordinary glass would block. In this type of experiment the laser beam bombards tiny, perfectly round pellets of matter. These implode, fusing their atomic nuclei and releasing energy. Below, an engineer adjusts a laser filter of the OMEGA system at the University of Rochester, New York. Laser fusion requires extremely accurate aiming and precise timing. At Rochester, 24 laser beams focus on a fuel pellet about a hundredth of an inch across, like the one pointed out below at left. The powerful pulse of laser radiation fired at the pellet lasts less than a hundred billionth of a second.*

TARGET PELLET

PELLET SHELL ON GLASS PROBE

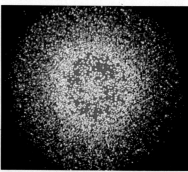

FUSION: X-RAY PHOTOGRAPH

GALAXY M 82, IN URSA MAJOR

## THE ASTRONOMERS'
## ELECTRONIC PAINT BOX

*From distant galaxies light speeds
earthward, reaching us bright enough
for study, yet far too faint for our eyes or
our photographic film to capture more
than a pastel hint of color. To re-create
what we could see if gifted with
supersensitive color vision, scientists
intensify the hues with the aid of
computers. The spiral galaxy at right
becomes a riot of splendor in the
enhanced image seen at far right. Here
older stars glow red; blue streaks show
where star formation takes place.
Above, a galaxy reveals to the unaided
film little of the events taking place at its
heart. But the computer-enhanced
image (above, right) clearly reveals the
turmoil caused by a galactic explosion
about a million and a half years ago.
The brilliant red glow comes from
gas moving outward from the site
of the explosion.*

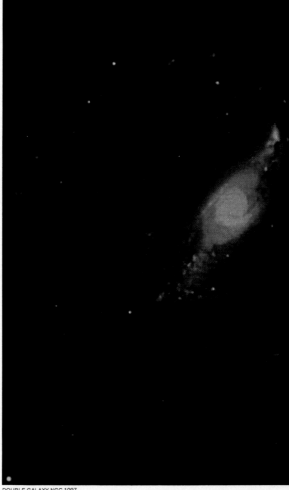

DOUBLE GALAXY NGC 1097

36

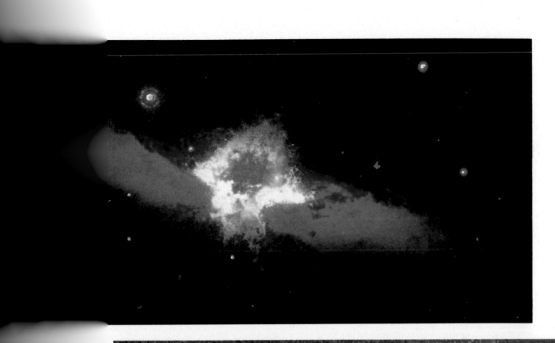

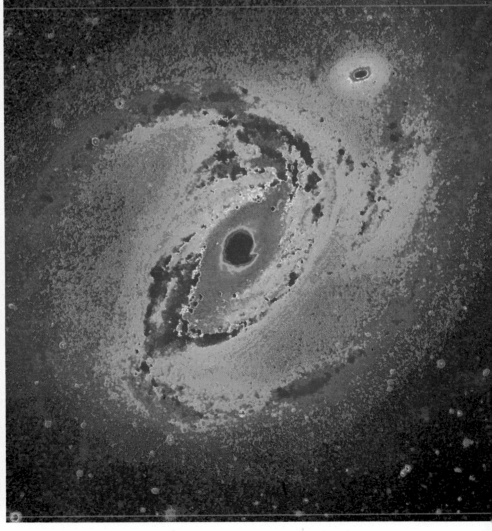

for gravitational attraction to gather them into clouds. After a billion years or so, however, expansion had cooled the gas enough that it could condense into clouds, and in turn the clouds could collapse into galaxies.

To a degree, the evolution of the universe can be seen—literally—by looking back into time. Comprehending that fact provided one of the earliest and most lasting thrills of my own career. For when we look at very distant objects, we do not see what is there now but rather what existed at the time the light we observe was emitted.

The speed of light is great, but finite—and measurable: 186,282 miles per second. Of the major galaxies our nearest neighbor is M 31, a fuzzy patch beyond the star constellation Andromeda and hence called the Andromeda galaxy; it is a little more than two million *light-years* from us. Since its light has traveled more than two million years to reach us, we are seeing the galaxy as it existed that many years ago. In cosmic terms, that is not such a long time.

For truly distant objects, the light may have been traveling for a considerable portion of the age of the universe. The most distant galaxies so studied, seen beyond the constellation Serpens of our galaxy, are ten billion light-years away. Ten billion years is more than twice the age of our earth, and about two-thirds the total age of the universe.

At the greatest distances from us are the quasars (short for quasi-stellar objects), enigmatic energy sources for which optical detail has only recently been discerned. But the light coming from the quasars has been lengthened to more than four times its original wavelength, because they are now four times as far away as when the light was emitted. The quasars were already so far away then that the light has had to travel about eight-tenths of the time the universe has existed in order to reach us!

Still other mysteries resolved in part by the theory of the big bang lie in the interplay of elementary particles and the forces between them. To place this great adventure in perspective, we must make a mighty leap. We must go from the largest to the smallest, from the all-but-invisible realm of distant galaxies to the completely unseen world of subatomic particles. In doing so, we will begin to see how interdependent are our investigations of these two regions, seemingly so remote from each other, and how much the efforts of astronomers and of physicists have become complementary.

Since antiquity, scholars have tried to define the fundamental substances of the universe. The ancient Greeks thought them to be earth, air, fire, and water; it seemed to them that the properties of one or a combination of those "elements" could describe anything. Many centuries later, scientists learned about the chemical elements, and found that all matter is composed of atoms. Then the atoms were found to be made up of even smaller components—protons, neutrons, and electrons.

The atom and its parts are so small that we need concrete comparisons to get some idea of their size.

Suppose that everything were magnified ten billion times, so that the head of a pin became as large as the planet earth is now. In that magnified world, an atom would be a fuzzy ball about six feet across. A swarm of electrons would orbit about a center. Deep in the heart of that swarm of electrons, which actually is mostly empty space, lies the nucleus, no bigger (even with all that magnification) than the tip of a sharp pencil. Yet from that tiny, extremely dense structure, protons and neutrons can be knocked out, one by one, demonstrating that each is a part of the nucleus.

I feel very fortunate in having been caught up in the drama connecting nuclear physics and astronomy. In the early 1950s my Ph.D. thesis adviser, William A. Fowler, was leading an experimental program in the structure of the atomic nucleus. His laboratory utilized a type of particle accelerator called a Van de Graaf generator—a larger version of a device commonly found in high-school science labs today. His generator accelerated protons to high velocities by an electrical push of about three million volts. The speeding protons then were allowed to collide with the nuclei of other atoms. By measuring the reactions and characteristics of particles knocked loose by the collisions, the researchers were attempting

*Clues to secrets of the universe, symbols march across a blackboard in the University of Texas office of physicist Steven Weinberg. His scientific interests range from galaxies to subatomic particles. In 1979 he shared the Nobel Prize in Physics. Twelve years earlier, Weinberg had developed a theory that explained the relationship between two of the four fundamental forces of nature. The theory showed that the two forces— the weak nuclear force that causes certain atomic nuclei to decay, and the electromagnetic force that holds electrons in orbit around nuclei— are actually aspects of the same phenomenon. In 1977 Weinberg's book* The First Three Minutes *interpreted the big-bang theory of the origin of the universe.*

to learn more about the nuclei themselves, particularly their behavior in an excited state.

Into Fowler's lab came Fred Hoyle, the famed British cosmologist who had proposed a steady-state model of the universe, and who was to form a fruitful collaboration with Fowler that would last for two decades. Hoyle was studying the carbon nucleus, and wondered whether it might have a previously undiscovered configuration that could break apart into three helium nuclei.

Hoyle reasoned that such a configuration, or excited state, must exist, with a predictable energy for the three helium nuclei, or else the stars would not be able to convert helium into carbon. If this fusion could not take place, he argued, carbon would not be nearly so common as we know it to be.

Fowler, an ebullient midwesterner turned Californian, remembers feeling some annoyance at this seemingly mystical line of reasoning, and wishing that "the crackpot would go away." But because of Hoyle's reputation and persistence, Fowler reluctantly agreed to a search by his colleague, Ward Whaling. To his astonishment the results exactly confirmed what Hoyle had predicted. It was the first time that a specific property of the nucleus of an atom had been accurately anticipated on the basis of an astronomical theory.

As Fowler declared later, "That was what finally hooked me on nuclear astrophysics." It was a fortunate turn for science. Fowler and Hoyle went on to elaborate the theory of nucleosynthesis—the production of other elements from hydrogen—in stars. Fowler built his laboratory into the world center for studying with accelerators the nuclear reactions believed to happen in the stellar furnaces.

The incident also inspired my own scientific life. As Fowler's graduate student I began a 15-year apprenticeship with him and with Hoyle, in Pasadena and in Cambridge, that brought me much excitement and joy.

Everyone is somewhat uncomfortable at first with the scope and complexity of the family of atomic nuclei. There are 92 naturally occurring elements—not all found on earth or in stable forms. They range *(Continued on page 46)*

# A STAR IS BORN OF COSMIC GAS AND DUST

*Glowing red, a cloud of hydrogen gas some 2,700 light-years from earth marks a birthplace of stars (right). Concentrations of dust show as dark streaks, in some places faintly tinged with blue reflected starlight. One such dark cloud gives the Cone Nebula (below) its most prominent feature. Drawn together by gravity, the gas and dust collapse into clumps.*
*The continued condensing of a clump raises its temperature; eventually a new star shines.*

REGION OF MONOCEROS, RIGHT

WOLF-RAYET STAR HD 56925

## NEBULA: EXPLOSION OR VIOLENT WIND?

*Helix Nebula (opposite) pushes outward as a vast cloud glowing with the red of nitrogen and hydrogen. Nuclear reactions within a star formed the heavier element from hydrogen. The star's outer layers blew away when an explosion or a "superwind" driven by radiation pressure overwhelmed the gravity that had held them in place. Above, powerful stellar winds speeding away from another massive star push before them cosmic gas and dust, forming a giant bubble.*

*PAGES 44-45: Wispy strands of interstellar gas, overtaken and compressed by the shock wave from a supernova, race across the sky of the southern hemisphere in the constellation Vela.*

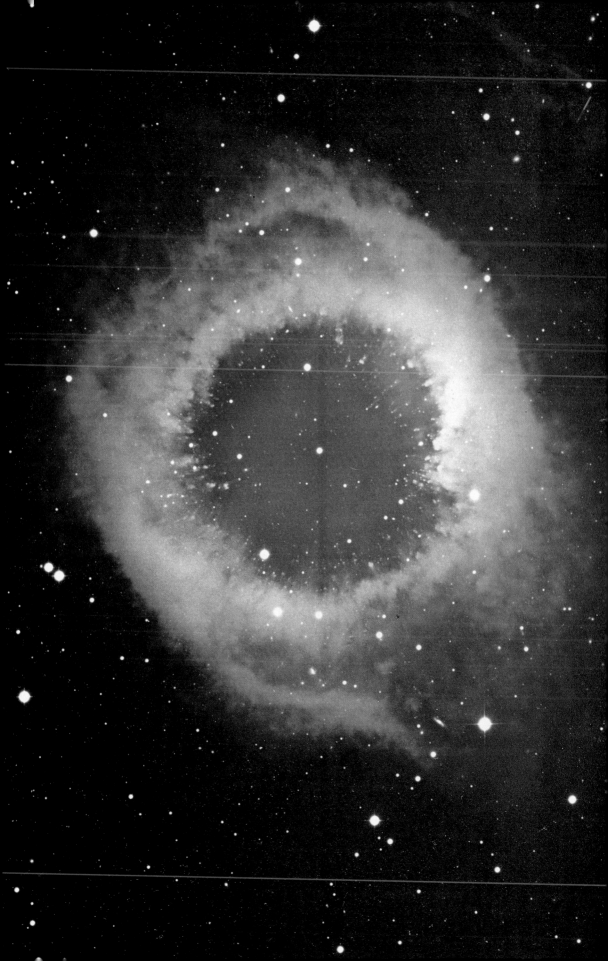

from hydrogen, whose atomic nucleus has a single proton and no neutron, to uranium, with a nucleus of 92 protons and 146 neutrons. Many elements have variant forms, called isotopes, containing the same number of protons but different numbers of neutrons. The total number of protons and neutrons determines the isotope's atomic mass.

Hydrogen has two abundant forms. The nucleus of an atom of ordinary hydrogen is a lone proton; one of its isotopes, called deuterium or heavy hydrogen, has a proton *and* a neutron. Both forms behave chemically as hydrogen, but deuterium has very different nuclear properties from those of hydrogen. It is from deuterium and a rare third isotope, tritium, that the thermonuclear hydrogen bomb derives its terrible power. On a more positive note, deuterium offers hope for an almost inexhaustible source of nuclear energy. Each cubic yard of seawater contains 30 grams of deuterium, whose fusion into helium could liberate five million kilowatt hours of electrical power—assuming technological problems of efficient conversion can be solved. And each cubic mile of ocean contains five billion times the amount of fuel in a cubic yard.

But hydrogen is only one of the elements. All told, the 92 elements have 353 natural isotopes. We know about how common each element—in fact, each isotope—is in the solar system, and, by inference, throughout our galaxy and the universe. One of the tasks of nuclear astrophysics is to attempt to learn why the relative abundances are as they are. For example, why is silicon 16 times as abundant as calcium? Scientists search for the answers to such questions within the atomic nucleus, and in the study of natural events where nuclear reactions commonly take place.

The centers of stars are giant thermonuclear reactors, fusing lighter elements into heavier ones. Stars usually don't explode, because such enormous gas spheres are held together by their own weight despite their high internal temperatures. The core of the sun is about 15 million degrees Kelvin, or 27 million degrees Fahrenheit. But so great is the mass of the sun, 330,000 times that of earth, that the overlying layers bear down on the core with a crushing pressure of two billion tons per square inch.

If similar reactions are attempted here on earth, it is of course necessary to find some other means to confine the hot gas. This confinement problem is a major obstacle to generating fusion power. The problem is not that a reactor might explode like a hydrogen bomb, for it would not, but rather that the gas loses its temperature to confining walls before it gets hot enough to complete the process and liberate any power.

The most promising devices, the tokamak and magnetic-mirror fusion reactors, confine the hot gas with a magnetic field so that it does not reach the walls. A major challenge has been to create a leakproof "magnetic bottle" from which the positively charged atoms cannot escape.

Another approach is to heat a pellet of fusion fuel suddenly with a burst of laser beams. The brief high temperature causes the pellet to be compressed sufficiently for fusion to occur, but on a small scale that can be controlled. On such research rests the possibility of obtaining clean, plentiful thermonuclear power for earth's growing energy needs.

In the hot, gaseous center of the sun there are no such difficulties, of course, and there hydrogen is constantly being fused into helium. But it was not an easy matter to determine by what nuclear reactions the fusion occurs. Many laboratory experiments were necessary to confirm the detailed reactions predicted by Hans Bethe—for which he was awarded the Nobel Prize in Physics in 1967.

I had the good luck to study one of these reactions as a graduate student under Fowler's guidance. Excited as usual, the professor had called me to his office to show me astronomical observations indicating that in some red giant stars the isotope carbon 13 is almost as abundant as carbon 12, even though on earth carbon 13 occurs only one-nineteenth as often. This made no sense if, as some thought, collisions with protons would destroy carbon 13 much more rapidly than carbon 12. Fowler suggested that I check the reaction with one of the laboratory Van de Graafs. As it turned out, my study resolved the apparent conflict by showing that earlier interpretations of the

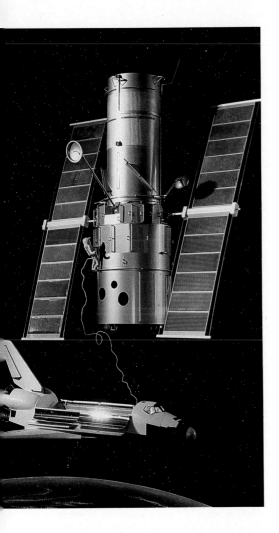

*Astronaut on a maintenance mission climbs aboard the Space Telescope in a scene modeled in miniature at a motion picture studio. Scheduled for launch by space shuttle in 1985, the 12-ton observatory will provide the clearest images of stars ever produced. Aiming the telescope at galaxies more than 13 billion light-years away, scientists expect to discover clues to the origins of the universe. Other early projects planned for the observatory include investigating the far reaches of our solar system and searching for planets around nearby stars.*

sketchy data had been incorrect, and that carbon 13 could not be rapidly destroyed within the stars.

Fleshing out the theory of the stellar furnaces, like many other recent developments in theoretical astronomy, was possible only with the aid of advanced computers. Their calculations show that a star undergoes a series of nuclear burning stages. The ashes of one stage become the fuel for the next as the temperature rises. The final composition of the universe as computed from the theory matches well the actual composition as we observe it. Thus it seems certain that the nuclei of the atoms on earth, except for those of hydrogen, were assembled as nuclear ashes in stellar reactors. We are made of cosmic fallout!

This seemed to me almost science fiction when I first heard of it as a young man of 22, but Willy Fowler made it reasonable by pointing out that even our own thermonuclear bomb explosions can create new nuclei. When the first hydrogen bomb was exploded on Eniwetok atoll in the Pacific in November 1952, the fallout contained a radioactive element, plutonium, that was not then known to exist naturally on earth, although it had been produced in 1940 at the cyclotron at Berkeley. Only very limited traces of the element have been found occurring naturally.

And of course, said Fowler, the explosions of stars are much more violent than any force we can release on earth. If a bomb can make plutonium, how much more can a supernova do! This latter point had been impressed on him by Fred Hoyle, who first developed the theory that some elements were assembled in supernova explosions.

This same framework of nuclear physics even enables us to determine how old the elements are. It was my good fortune to discover such an atomic clock in 1962. I was developing a theory to explain how the heavy elements had been formed. But I was concerned about a troublesome point where the theory did not work. One isotope of the element osmium was almost twice as abundant as the theory indicated it ought to be.

After worrying about this inconsistency a good deal, I noticed that one form of rhenium, another element, actually decays very slowly and eventually becomes osmium. It dawned on me that enough time must have elapsed since the first creation of elements in stars for part of the earth's rhenium to have decayed into osmium—thus making the latter more abundant. Carrying out the necessary calculations, I found that the synthesis of rhenium nuclei began at least ten billion years ago—more than twice the age of our solar system. It was a thrilling discovery, confirming an important aspect of the history of the universe.

In the old-fashioned view of nuclear physics, an atom was understood to be made up of some combination of three kinds of particles: protons, electrons, and neutrons. Protons and neutrons were parts of the atom's nucleus; the electrons orbited around the nucleus. Each proton carried a positive electric charge; the neutrons had no charge; and each electron carried a negative charge.

The nearest electrons typically were at a distance 10,000 times the size of the nucleus itself. Thus, if the atom were enlarged so the nucleus became the size of an orange, the nearest electrons would orbit about a mile away.

It was necessary to envision two different forces to account for this structure. The electrons are held in their orbits around the nucleus by an electromagnetic attraction that is relatively weak. To hold the fast-moving protons and neutrons within the much smaller nucleus demands a force a hundred times stronger than the electromagnetic force. This came to be known as the nuclear force or "strong force."

A third force was needed to explain such changes as neutron decay. An isolated neutron changes into a proton. The decay is accompanied by the creation of two particles—an electron and something scientists named the neutrino. Since it takes a relatively long time for neutrons to decay, it is apparent that the force that causes the change is weak. Accordingly, this came to be known as the "weak force."

But even before the physicists had fully explained this tidy arrangement of three forces (electromagnetic, strong, and weak) and four particles (proton, neutron, electron, and neutrino), they re-alized the world of elementary particles was more complicated than that. In the 1930s, investigations of cosmic rays penetrating our atmosphere led to the discovery of mesons and other particles. When the age of accelerators arrived in the 1950s and '60s, a revolution in high-energy physics took place. Using more and more powerful machines, scientists identified more than a hundred particles; and the vocabulary necessary to distinguish them kept growing: hadrons, baryons, muons, pions.

All these particles are very short-lived, and in 1964 Murray Gell-Mann and Georg Zweig independently suggested that all are composites of even smaller particles, which Gell-Mann whimsically named quarks. Today some physicists believe two groups of particles—quarks and leptons—are the fundamental units of matter. Others, however, have already started looking for "sub-quarks."

Combinations of quarks form the particles that respond to the "strong" or nuclear force—including our familiar protons and neutrons. The other category, leptons, includes the particles that respond to the weak or the electromagnetic force—among them the electrons and neutrinos.

The terminology of the world of quarks suggests a wonderland of imagination. Appropriately enough, Nobel laureate Gell-Mann took the quarks' name from a line in James Joyce's novel *Finnegans Wake:* "Three quarks for Muster Mark!"

To describe the several kinds of quarks, their scientist sponsors have organized them by "color" and "flavor." Quarks come in three "colors"—often labeled red, blue, and green, though the choice seems to lie with the individual. These have nothing to do with visual colors, of course, but instead remind physicists of certain characteristics each group possesses. For each color, five "flavors" of quarks have been identified, and researchers are so sure there are actually six that they have already assigned names to all six: *up* and *down, strange* and *charm, beauty* and *truth.* (Ironically, *truth* is the quark that has not yet been experimentally verified.)

Scientists in attendance at the Aspen Center for Physics in Colorado several

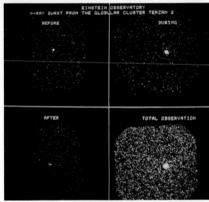

*Gesturing toward a painting of the Einstein Observatory, the X-ray astronomy satellite he designed, Dr. Riccardo Giacconi calls the observatory his "telephone line to nature." Giacconi presently directs the Space Telescope Science Institute at Johns Hopkins University in Baltimore, Maryland. He and his colleagues study the emissions associated with such little-understood celestial objects as black holes and neutron stars. The four X-ray television images show a burster, one of the rarest of the phenomena observed by the satellite: Within less than a minute, an object smaller than 30 miles across emits a sudden burst of X-ray energy more powerful than all the energy our sun gives off in a week.*

years ago recount a hilarious parody on the quark terminology. In the skit Gell-Mann acted out the role of a "mad scientist" who not only recommended the entire slate of curious names but also proposed that predicted particles be searched out by chasing tiny protons around a big ring with buffaloes in the center. This reference to the Fermi National Accelerator Laboratory in Illinois, where bison do in fact graze near the large accelerator rings, brought down the house—and was followed by the arrival of men in white coats who hauled away the protesting Gell-Mann.

Except for the leptons, all of the more than one hundred known subatomic particles seem to be constructed from quarks. The beauty of the theory is not just that known particles can be described in terms of these building blocks, but that the combinations that can be made with them correspond to the known particles. In other words, only those particles *do* exist that the theory says *should* exist. Furthermore, particle theory now has great success in calculating which particles will decay into what other particles, and how fast the decay will be.

Obtaining and interpreting data about elementary particles has become ever more difficult and expensive. Experiments now are conducted on large, costly accelerators after years of planning. They involve sizable teams of physicists, often from several universities or research laboratories. One such institution is the Stanford Linear Accelerator Center, where a two-mile-long vacuum tube is equipped with giant microwave power tubes that accelerate electrons and positrons almost to the speed of light. Such experiments show that the electron bounces off three centers of mass within the proton. These chunks are believed to be the quarks, held together inside the proton by the strong nuclear force.

All these particles—projectiles and targets alike—are of course far too small to be observed directly. Various instruments have been designed to detect their traces and enable these to be photographed or otherwise recorded for careful study. For example, one detector is the "proportional chamber," filled with gas. A charged particle—say, a projectile electron angling  *(Continued on page 54)*

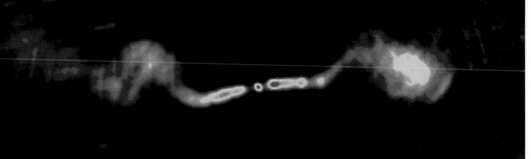

RADIO SOURCE 3C 449

*Double rainbow arcs above a bank of antennas of the Very Large Array radio telescope sprawling across the desert near Socorro, New Mexico. Its 27 dish antennas, electronically linked, ride on 38 miles of railroad track laid out in the shape of a Y to permit varied positioning. Clustered together, they record the large-scale structure of cosmic radio sources; spread far apart, they capture fine detail. This giant instrument enables astronomers for the first time to produce radio maps more detailed than the images obtained by the best ground-based optical telescopes. Thus the VLA will complement the forthcoming Space Telescope. Above, a technician adjusts a television monitor —an "eyepiece" of the telescope—in the control building. The TV screen not only displays images but also adds color to highlight selected data. At top, a VLA radio map shows jets of energy streaming from the center of a galaxy 350 million light-years away.*

51

# BLACK HOLES: GRAVITY SO GREAT NO LIGHT ESCAPES

*At Cambridge, England, Dr. Stephen Hawking explores the universe with his wide-ranging intellect. Struck by Lou Gehrig's disease in 1962, Hawking continues his research, dictating page after page of complex mathematical formulas to an assistant. Meetings with his university colleagues (below) vibrate with mental exercise. His field of theory: black holes—enigmatic concentrations of matter formed when a star burns away its nuclear fuel and collapses into an object so dense its gravity allows no light to escape, thus rendering itself invisible. A black hole may exist at the center of galaxy M 87 (bottom), seen through a telescope at left and in a computer-enhanced image at right. Near its center stars circle at great speed, as if attracted by immense gravity from a compact object otherwise undetectable.*

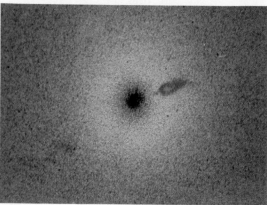

away after hitting a target proton—leaves a track of ionized atoms, which then yield their information in a form that can be read by a computer.

In all experiments where a high-energy electron beam hits a target at rest, a difficulty arises from the very high speed of the electron. In effect, its velocity makes it so massive that when it hits its target, electron and target tend to move along together, and only a small fraction of the electron's energy contributes to the force of the collision.

The difficulty can be imagined as that of a fly, complete with tiny catcher's mitt, trying to catch a baseball in midair. The fly might think he catches it, but it would be more accurate to say that the baseball catches the fly, because both now move with, and in the flight path of, the baseball.

Consider how different would be the fate of the fly were he to ride on a second baseball whizzing toward the first at the same speed. The physicists at Stanford utilized this very principle by building storage rings. After acceleration, the electrons and their target particles are injected into a ring 1.5 miles around. There they move in a circular orbit maintained by magnetic fields. The trick is that they move in opposite directions. When they meet head-on, all their combined energy contributes to the force of the collision.

The recent work of two groups illustrates the interplay between the quark theory and such accelerators and storage rings. In the 1970s, Burton Richter and his colleagues at Stanford began to search for new combinations of quarks. At that time only three quarks were known, but there had been speculation about a fourth, named "charm" by the theorists. Eventually Richter and his team found a new particle that seemed to contain the predicted quark.

As frequently happens in science, another team—this one led by Samuel Ting of the Massachusetts Institute of Technology—was making an independent search at Brookhaven National Laboratory in New York. This group also found the particle, at virtually the same time. The discoveries rocked the world of physics, demonstrating again the soundness of the quark idea and identifying specifically the fourth quark. Richter and

*Physicist Murray Gell-Mann pores over mathematical papers in his office in Pasadena. The California Institute of Technology professor won the Nobel Prize in Physics in 1969 for his explanation of relationships among the hundreds of subatomic particles discovered during the preceding two decades. Gell-Mann showed that still smaller particles, which he named "quarks," would form various combinations to make up most of the particles researchers had identified.*

Ting were awarded, almost immediately, the 1976 Nobel Prize in Physics.

Particle physicists quite naturally want to continue their research at higher energies. Richter has advocated a "linear collider" as the most practical way of reaching such energies. Such a facility might cost 110 million dollars, raising an interesting question of value. It sounds like a huge sum to enable a small band of physicists to embark on an esoteric search for an elusive particle. On the other hand, it does not seem like a very high price for understanding the ultimate structure of matter. Will new leptons and new quarks be revealed at higher energies, or is six of each to be the final number? We cannot now predict the answer.

The force of gravity differs from the other three particle forces—electromagnetic, strong, and weak—in profound ways. This force is so incredibly weak that a large mass is needed before the force is even noticed. The attraction between two marbles is so slight that they show no tendency to roll toward each other when placed on a level tabletop, even though each marble contains a million billion billion atoms. Consider, then, how weak must be the attraction between two atoms!

Whether or not it was a falling apple that triggered the idea, Isaac Newton in the 17th century realized that it is the huge mass of the earth that makes its gravity so evident. Gravity finds a natural and vital role in the realm of astronomy, where very large bodies exist.

Gravity is the prime mover in the universe, from the astronomer's point of view. In our own solar system the planets circle the sun, held in their orbits by gravitational force.

And what of the sun itself? The attraction of each portion of that body inward toward its great mass keeps the sun from blowing apart, despite the huge pressures and multimillion-degree temperatures within.

Observations confirm that new stars are continually being born in our Milky Way galaxy. Great clouds of cold gas and dust float about the galaxy, gradually being pulled in on themselves by their own gravity. Ultimately the gravitation becomes so strong that the cloud or some portion of it collapses inward to form a star.

This process can be seen now in the giant clouds of the Orion nebula. Once begun, the collapse stops only when the rising temperature turns on a nuclear reaction and builds internal pressure strong enough to offset the compressing force of gravity. Then a new star comes into being. Such stars, many of which are similar to our own sun, orbit the center of the galaxy for the rest of their lives.

And what of the origins of galaxies, the countless islands of stars like our Milky Way that populate the visible universe? They appear to have formed from even greater clouds of gas, cooling and coagulating in the aftermath of the big bang. In many cases they assume the flattened form of majestic spirals.

Everywhere, at every scale, the drama of the universe is repeated again and again. And it is the force of gravity that causes a universe composed fundamentally of gas to contract to ever more bewildering forms.

It was a shocking experience for me to learn that Newton's beautiful theory of gravity is not totally correct. It was strange indeed to study the theory diligently in college, and then to discover in graduate school that for complex conceptualizing it had been superseded by a better one—Einstein's General Theory of Relativity.

How can the profound differences between Newton and Einstein be summarized? Einstein's revolution began in 1905 with his Special Theory of Relativity, encompassing the idea that space and time cannot be thought of as separate entities. They are intrinsically linked, and it is only the combination of the two that will appear the same to two observers who move relative to one another.

Newton had thought of space and time as having independent and absolute meanings. Einstein proposed curved combinations of space and time; he argued that both light and matter travel on the shortest path through such space-time, and insisted that mass and energy cause the curvature. As astronomers look outward, they see bizarre puzzles—from the expansion of space to suspected black holes—that can be explained with the aid of Einstein's concepts.

55

The large red shift of light from quasars places them very far from us. To be bright enough to look like an ordinary star at such a distance, the source must have a power output at least a hundred times as bright as a galaxy containing a hundred billion stars. The shocker is that such fierce power seems to emerge, not from the area of a huge galaxy, but from a tiny region that is not much larger than our solar system.

Especially exciting has been the discovery of multiple-image quasars. Such images were predicted by Einstein's interpretation of space-time. Several cases have been found in which a barely detectable galaxy located between us and a quasar causes space to curve around it on either side. In effect, light from the quasar takes two different paths. This causes the quasar to appear doubled—like two identical quasars close to each other in the sky with the galaxy between them. Recently—even more exotic—a triple-image quasar was sighted.

Einstein had recognized the possibility of such multiple images, but in an article published in 1936 he concluded "there is no great chance of observing this phenomenon." For all his brilliance, Einstein could not foresee the great advances that would allow astronomers to study vastly more distant objects than they could in his day.

Instead of photographing an object, astronomers now can record electronically individual photons, or increments of light, making it possible to "observe" objects too faint to be detected on film. This technology uses computers to produce images in color on a television screen. The astronomer can then analyze these images in ways not possible by studying photographs alone.

Studies of galaxies have indicated that certain ones may be related to the mystery of the quasar. Although most galaxies are stately and serene, some show signs of violent activity in a small central region called the nucleus. These are called "active galaxies."

An active galaxy has an intensely bright nucleus—so bright that it may have to be masked when the observer wants to see the remainder of the galaxy. Stars move extraordinarily fast near this center, as if a strong gravitational force propels them. The light from the nucleus changes rapidly, in months or even days, so we must conclude that the massive center is no larger than the distance light could travel in that brief time.

Think of it this way: An output of light equal to ten billion suns comes from a central region whose diameter is a great deal less than the distance from our sun to the nearest star, four light-years away. And that vast output changes dramatically within a month or so.

This behavior is so similar to that of quasars that many astronomers have come to believe quasars represent the early violent stages in the evolution of active galaxies. The quasars are so far away that the light we see now is extremely ancient. The active galaxies have evolved to a later stage, visible to us in that form because their light has not had so far to travel. They may therefore be former quasars, whose violence has dimmed over their long galactic lifetimes.

The road signs of physics for interpreting such behavior point toward the existence of supermassive "black holes" in the nuclei of active galaxies. The hypothesis of the black hole follows from Einstein's space-time description of gravity. An object of sufficient mass causes light to curve as it passes by. If enough mass is concentrated in a small enough volume, its gravitational force would be so great that the curved light could actually orbit the mass. Nothing could escape, not even light. Such an object by itself would only absorb, not emit, light; that is, it would be black, invisible. From without, one would see no structure, only evidence of a fierce gravitational attraction: a ring of bright light around the black hole, light emitted by matter being squeezed into a tight orbit. That matter could reach extreme velocities, so that collisions among particles would generate intense radiation.

The nucleus of the nearby giant radio galaxy M 87 seems to have a black hole that yearly consumes the equivalent of several suns. The great vortex of matter crushing toward the hole is believed by many to explain M 87's dramatic jet, discovered in 1918 by astronomer H. D. Curtis, and similar jets of matter detected near the centers of other active galaxies.

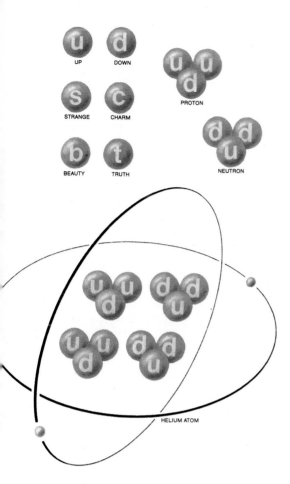

UP DOWN

STRANGE CHARM

PROTON

BEAUTY TRUTH

NEUTRON

HELIUM ATOM

*Fundamental building blocks of the atomic nucleus, quarks combine to make up almost all subatomic particles, including protons and neutrons. Their whimsical names serve as distinctive labels: "up" and "down"; "strange" and "charm"; "beauty" and "truth." Two "up" quarks and a "down" quark form a proton; two "downs" and an "up" make a neutron. Two protons and two neutrons, orbited by two electrons, make up an atom of helium. To fit the diagram onto the page, the artist had to place the orbits of the electrons much too close to the nucleus. If actually drawn to the same scale as the protons and neutrons, the nearest electron would circle about 500 yards away.*

The compactness of the black hole is almost impossible to imagine. Its size depends upon how much mass lies within it. For a mass equal to that of the earth, the black hole would be about half an inch in diameter! Even at that size, it would attract an object within a hundred miles with a force equal to 2,000 times the gravity of earth.

For a mass equal to that of the sun, the diameter of the black hole would be about 4 miles. The earth, even Jupiter, could easily be drawn into orbit around such a body.

For a mass equal to that of five billion suns, which is the estimate for the black hole in M 87, the diameter would be about 18 billion miles, or three times that of Neptune's orbit.

Such staggering concepts have been repeatedly clarified for us by Cambridge University cosmologist Stephen Hawking, who has also won the world's admiration for exerting his brilliant leadership despite the crippling Lou Gehrig's disease from which he suffers. Confined to a motorized wheelchair, unable to write by hand, barely able to speak, he has nevertheless contributed profoundly to the evolving theory of black holes. He has even shown that, in one sense, black holes are not *totally* black after all. By combining the theories of quantum mechanics and general relativity, he has found that a black hole emits—randomly and very rarely—energetic particles near its boundary.

Commenting on Hawking's remarkable ability to marshal seemingly boundless intellectual energy in the discouragement of disability, a British Broadcasting Corporation narrator said: "With a physical handicap, you can't afford a psychological one. Although the gentle gravity of the earth confines him to a wheelchair, in his mind he comprehends the gravity of a black hole."

Astronomers have long noticed in the motion of galaxies evidence of much more mass than can be seen. This enigma, one of the most puzzling in astronomy, has come to be called "the missing mass problem." Astrophysicist Gary Steigman prefers to call it "the missing light problem," because there is evidence for the presence of mass that is not shining. Hawking has speculated on a

## END OF THE LINE FOR SPEEDING ELECTRONS

*Gigantic detection devices dominate a laboratory at the Stanford Linear Accelerator Center south of San Francisco. Here microwaves accelerate electrons down a vacuum tube two miles long. Traveling almost at the speed of light, the electrons smash into nuclear*

targets near the end of the slender copper tube. Instruments angling away on either side of the tube detect and measure subnuclear particles as they scatter. Opposite: Dr. Burton Richter, technical director of the center, stands watch in an experiment control room. In 1976 he and Dr. Samuel Ting of the Massachusetts Institute of Technology shared the Nobel Prize in Physics. Independently each had discovered a new particle that showed the need for a fourth type of quark, called "charm," to describe the structure of matter.

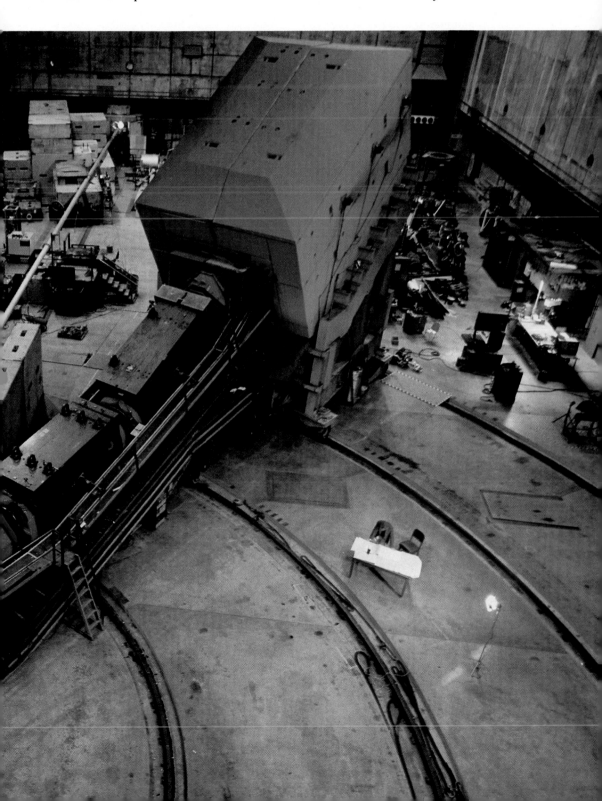

universe with enough black holes to account for this invisible mass.

It is not necessary to turn to other galaxies to find evidence of black holes. Perhaps the best example of all lies in our own Milky Way, in a highly variable source of X rays called Cygnus X-1. Here we observe the evidence of an invisible object, containing at least six times the mass of our sun, in a mutual orbit with a relatively normal giant star. The two move about each other like the weighted ends of a tumbling dumbbell. Apparently gaseous material is pulled away from the normal star and spirals down into the unseen companion, emitting X rays from the crushing turmoil near the vortex. X-ray-observing satellites orbiting the earth have gathered information on Cygnus X-1 that has not yet been completely analyzed. Astrophysicists have already concluded, however, that the invisible companion has too great a mass to be a white dwarf or a neutron star—the other known "final states" of stellar matter. It must be a black hole.

One of those final states cannot be avoided when a star begins to run out of nuclear fuel. As it cools, the gravitational force becomes dominant and the star begins to contract. If the star's mass is not more than 1.4 times that of the sun, the internal pressure generated by its confined electrons will be able to balance the gravitational force when the star has shrunk to a size similar to that of the earth. This balance, astrophysicist Subrahmanyan Chandrasekhar realized, is actually a demonstration of Einstein's Special Theory of Relativity combined with the so-called "Pauli exclusion principle," initially defined by the Austrian physicist Wolfgang Pauli to explain why individual atoms do not collapse. I find it amazing and thrilling that something so massive as a star could also be prevented from collapse by the effect of this same principle. The white dwarf stars that result are among the most numerous in the sky.

But if the stellar mass is greater than that of 1.4 suns, even the "exclusion-principle" pressure of the electrons cannot resist the compression of gravity. The inner part of the star suddenly collapses—within seconds—down to an object only about ten miles in diameter, while the outer part is blown away in a titanic explosion we call a supernova.

During the abrupt collapse, electrons and protons combine to create neutrons. The pressure does not become great enough to balance the crush of gravity until the ball of neutrons reaches a fantastic density—16 billion tons per cubic inch on the average, perhaps a hundred times that in the very center. This is a neutron star, a remarkable object predicted by physicists in the 1930s and now observed in the center of several supernova remnants, such as the Crab Nebula.

More than three hundred of these neutron stars have been detected by radio and X-ray astronomers. The intense shrinking process causes the star to rotate much more rapidly—many times per second—just as an ice skater spins faster as she pulls in her arms. Intense radio waves are emitted from two regions on or near the rapidly spinning neutron star, resulting in repetitive radio pulses. In 1967 Jocelyn Bell and Anthony Hewish at Cambridge University discovered the radio pulses, from objects now called pulsars, and opened new frontiers in both astronomy and physics.

If we assume a star whose mass is greater than that of three suns, even the neutrons provide insufficient pressure. After its lifelong struggle against the pull of gravity, such a star finally will lose decisively. It will collapse forever, we believe, into a black hole.

Of the challenges still facing those involved in particle physics, one of the most intriguing is the attempt to construct a "grand unified theory" that explains all four known forces—electromagnetic, strong, weak, and gravitational. Already the interactions of the weak and electromagnetic forces have been synthesized in the concept of an "electroweak force" advanced by John Ward, Abdus Salam, Sheldon Glashow, and Steven Weinberg. The latter three shared a Nobel prize in 1979 for their work on that achievement. Other theories have been proposed in the effort to unify those forces with the strong nuclear force; but it is still too early to know how the new arguments will fare in the crossfire of critique and test.

Nonetheless, scientists have speculated on the consequences of such a unified theory. If these speculations hold up, the details the theory supplies will explain one of nature's greatest mysteries—the stability of matter.

Certain experiments already begun may soon clarify these ideas. The average proton is thought to live an inconceivably long time, but is expected eventually to decay. This has never been observed; but if a huge number of protons are watched—as in a large, still body of water—there is a chance of seeing at least a few decay. In their search, scientists are now monitoring millions of gallons of water in several mines deep underground. Equally curious and potentially significant experiments are under way in other quarters.

So we stand, poised perhaps on the threshold of one of the great moments in the history of civilization. We are closer than ever before to understanding the puzzles of the existence of matter and its fundamental composition. So unprecedented is this situation that one of the most powerful thinkers of today, black-hole expert Stephen Hawking, has written a short book entitled, *Is the End in Sight for Theoretical Physics?*

Hawking cannot give the answer; but the fact that he would seriously ask the question reflects the simultaneous euphoria and astonishment of the world of theoretical physics.

History, of course, teaches caution. After Sir Isaac Newton's discoveries in the 17th century, some scholars thought that the future of physics would be limited to filling in the details of Newton's brilliant theories—none of which proved totally correct. No doubt today, too, there remain questions that have not yet even been conceived.

It is sobering to remember that our minds, as part of the universe, also operate by natural laws. It would be wondrous, indeed, if a small but admirable natural computer, the human brain, should be able to comprehend the entire universe. Albert Einstein's optimistic remark returns to us: " The most incomprehensible thing about the world is that it is comprehensible." In the human individual, one indeed finds a small part of creation trying to understand the whole. A small, cooled cinder has learned to ponder its origin.

*Quark hunter William Fairbank adjusts the delicate apparatus he believes has yielded evidence that single quarks exist in nature. The device levitates metal spheres, about the size of the tip of a ballpoint pen, with magnets. Detectors then measure with great accuracy the electrical charge of the suspended spheres. Dr. Fairbank and his collaborators have found that certain of the balls show a charge just one-third that of a single electron—a condition that would result from the presence of a single quark. Some scientists have expressed reservations about his conclusions. Meanwhile, the Fairbank group continues the quest in a basement laboratory at Stanford University.*

## PROTONS RIDE A MAGNETIZED MERRY-GO-ROUND

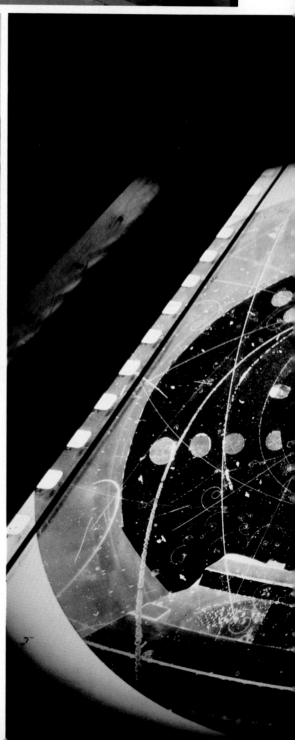

*Examining an enlarged negative, a technician studies tracks of subatomic particles created at the Fermi National Accelerator Laboratory 30 miles west of Chicago. Here magnets like the red and blue ones at left direct protons through a circular vacuum tube four miles in circumference. Sped along by radio waves, the protons race around the ring some 50,000 times a second before smashing into their nuclear targets. Meanwhile, bison from the laboratory's herd graze on pasturelands near the ring.*

PAGES 64-65: *Dr. Leon Lederman, director of the laboratory, ponders a technical paper. On the blackboard, budget figures for the institution overlay a schematic outline of the accelerator.*

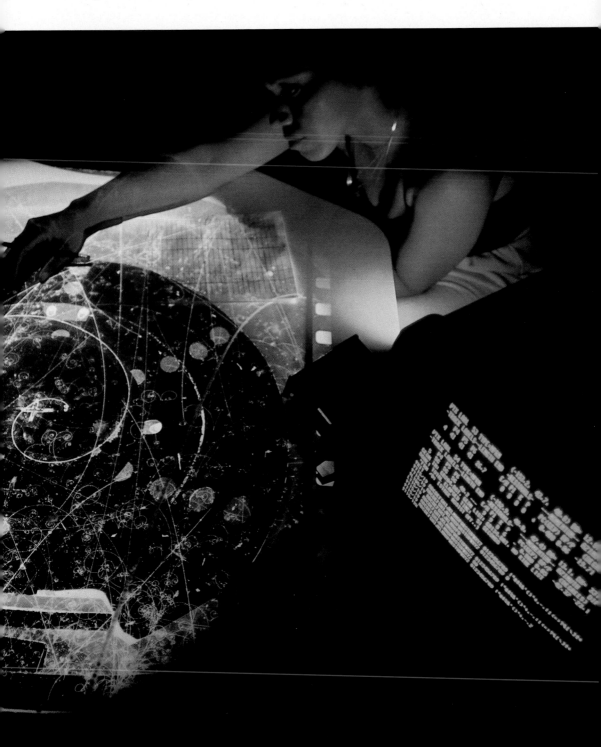

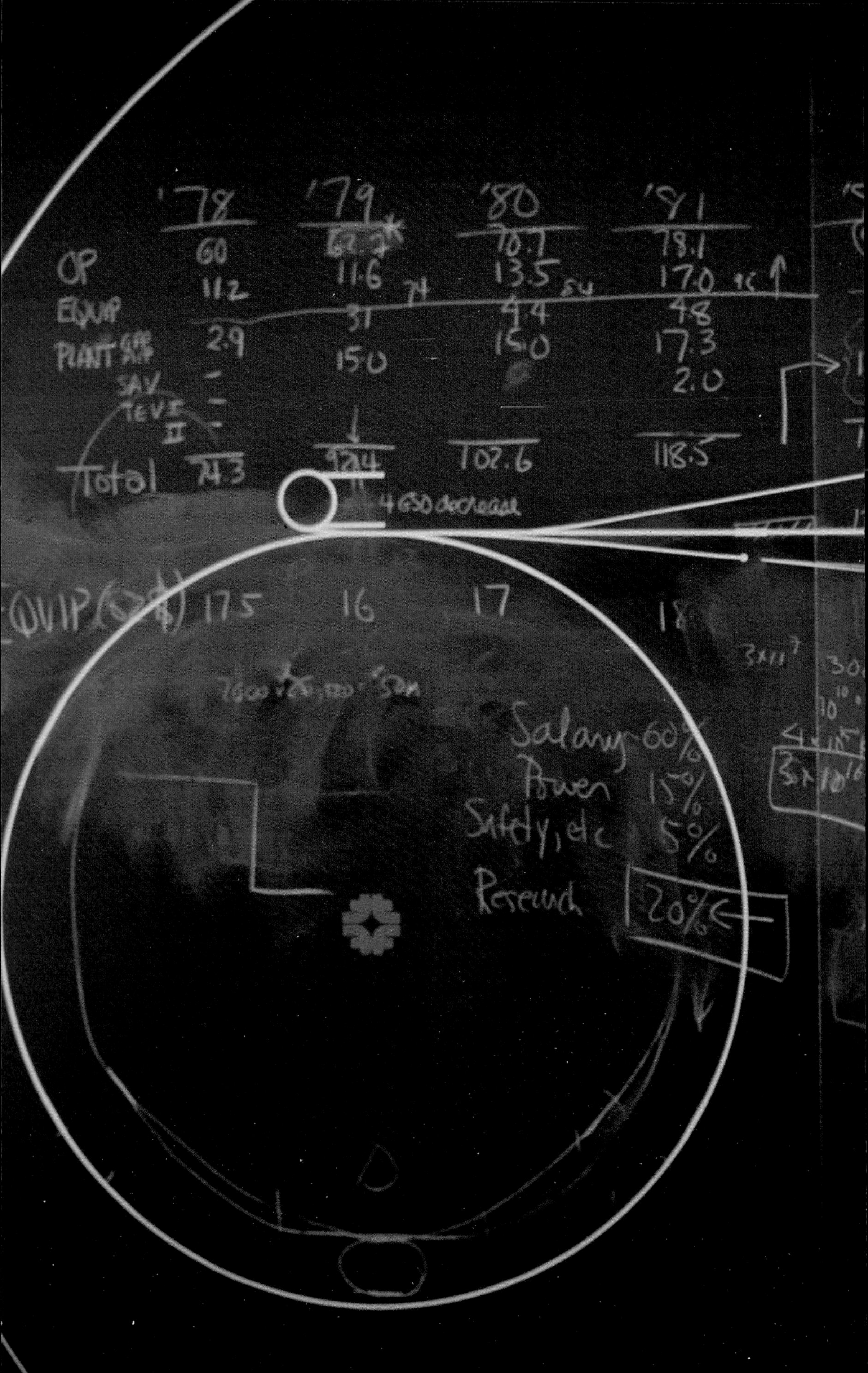

|        | '78 | '79 | '80 | '81 |
|--------|-----|-----|-----|-----|
| OP     | 60  | 62.2* | 70.7 | 78.1 |
| EQUIP  | 11.2 | 11.6 | 13.5 | 17.0 |
| PLANT SER | 2.9 | 31 | 4.4 | 48 |
| SAV    |     | 15.0 | 15.0 | 17.3 |
| TEV I  | —   |     |     | 2.0 |
| II     | —   |     |     |     |
| Total  | 74.3 | 124 | 102.6 | 118.5 |

4 650 decrease

EQUIP (OR $) 175    16    17    18

3×11

7600 728,700 50n

Salary 60%
Power 15%
Safety, etc 5%
Research 20% ←

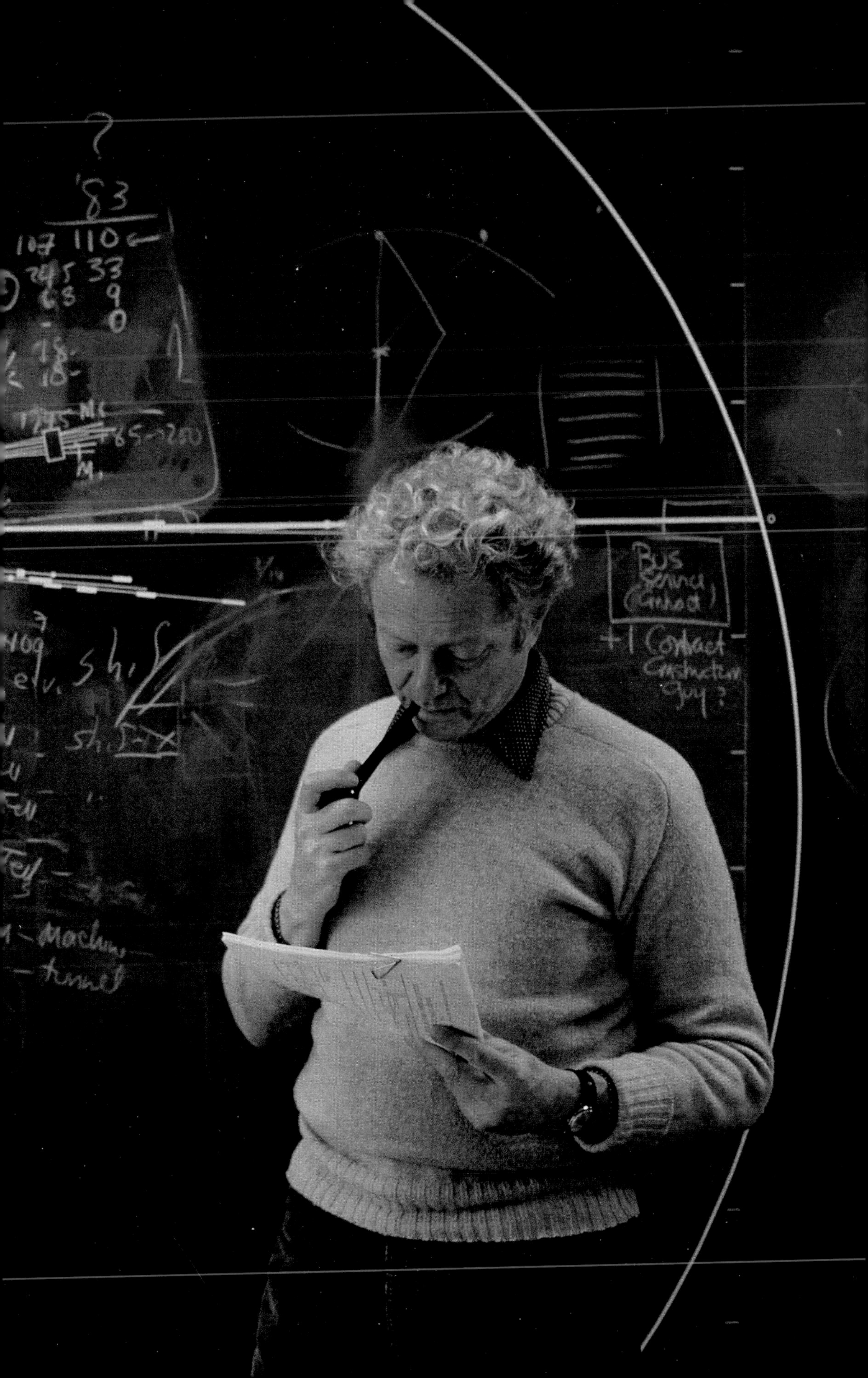
'83
BUS

# THE FAMILY OF THE SUN

*By* BRADFORD A. SMITH, *Ph. D.*
*Professor of Planetary Sciences,*
*The University of Arizona*

Like a tiny island in some cosmic sea, the solar system lies isolated and far removed from even the nearest of its celestial neighbors. From our own myopic perspective as we edge across the threshold of space exploration, the solar system seems immense. But from elsewhere in the galaxy, our sun would appear as an ordinary star, affording no hint that it is actually surrounded by a number of small, dark worlds, one of them an abode for living creatures—the planet earth.

Although this average, middle-aged star of ours is composed mostly of the light gases hydrogen and helium, it contains almost 99.9 percent of all matter in the solar system, and thus forms the gravitational hub about which the other bodies orbit. The planets, nine in all and ranging in size from diminutive Pluto to gigantic Jupiter, are made up of various substances. The solid planets of the inner group, including the earth, are mainly silicates and metals. The giants of the outer solar system are huge spheres consisting principally of hydrogen and helium. (Pluto, as we shall see, is a special case.)

Circling most of the planets are smaller, solid bodies called satellites, composed either of rock or, in the outer solar system, mixtures of rock and ice. The latest census of known satellites totals nearly fifty; of these, only three are found in the inner solar system—our own moon and *(Continued on page 72)*

*Pure, unblemished fire, Aristotle called the sun 2,300 years ago. Today's technology allows earthbound instruments to scan its surface, recording surging solar flares. Energy from this sphere of hydrogen and helium radiates throughout our solar system.*

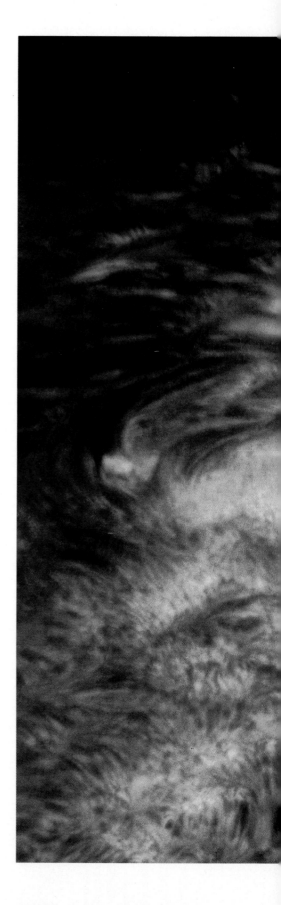

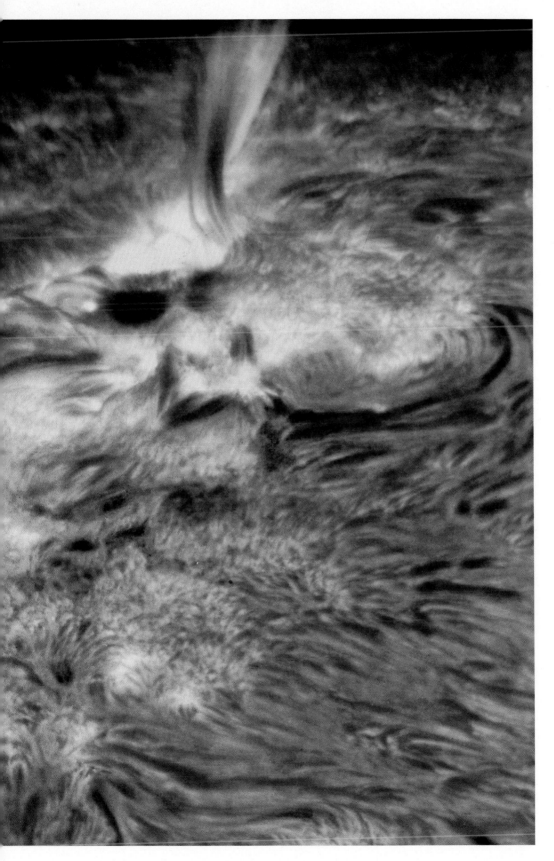

# OUR STABLE, VIOLENT STAR

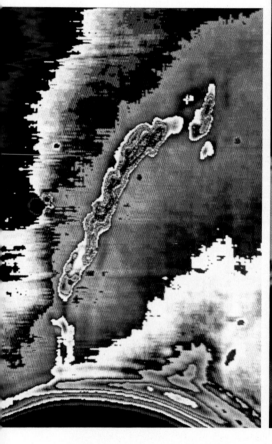

In a brilliant display of solar power, a prominence leaps hundreds of thousands of miles into the sun's corona. Lasting only a few hours, an erupting prominence contains hundreds of millions of tons of matter. Despite its basic stability, the sun displays constant surface activity that follows cycles averaging 11 years.

At the peak, violent magnetic storms associated with increased prevalence of sunspots, prominences, and flares rack the sun's surface. Anticipating such a period of "solar maximum," scientists in 1980 launched the earth-orbiting satellite Solar Max to record such disturbances; it took the photograph at left. In the

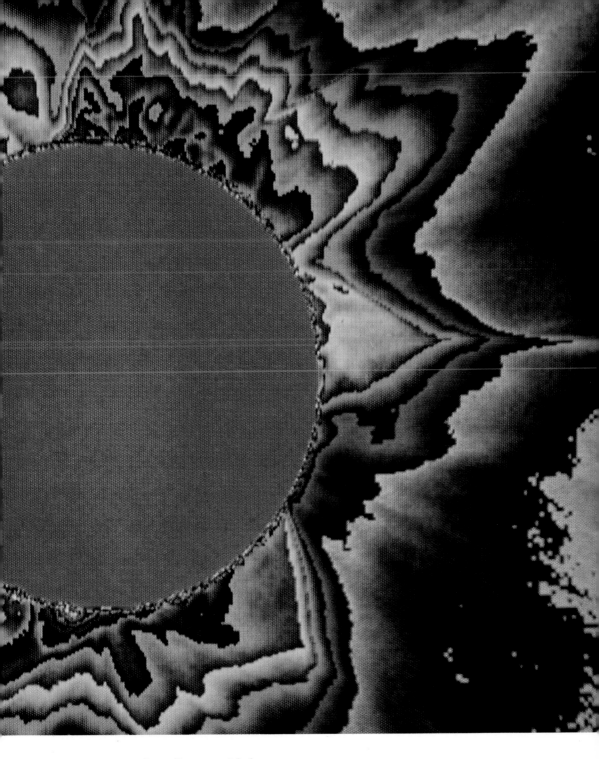

*same year, a solar eclipse provided an excellent opportunity to study the faint halo of gases usually obscured by the sun's bright disk. Made during the eclipse, the computer-enhanced image above uses assigned colors to denote different levels of brightness, and thus of density of material in the corona.*

# THE ORIGIN
# OF STAR SYSTEMS

*Out of the chaos created by a supernova,
or exploding massive star, new star
systems arise. Scientists theorize that
our own solar system may have formed
from the death throes of a supernova in
a spiral arm of our galaxy (above).
Nearly five billion years ago, its ejected
shell hurtled through space, sweeping up
material in the way and leaving in its
wake intensely hot, rarefied gases that
emitted X rays, shown as blue in the
painting at right. Many thousands of
years after the explosion, the blast
wave's forefront collides with a cold dark
cloud, its edge defined by a thin filament
glowing in the red light of hydrogen.
Behind this front, gases cooling after
impact stretch in a band of multicolored
segments produced by varying densities
and temperatures. The cool, dense,
orange pockets hold star potential. The
wave of debris further compresses these
regions. In time, gravity will pull the
clouds of gas and dust into spinning
disks, the stellar-system forerunners
called protostars and protoplanets.*

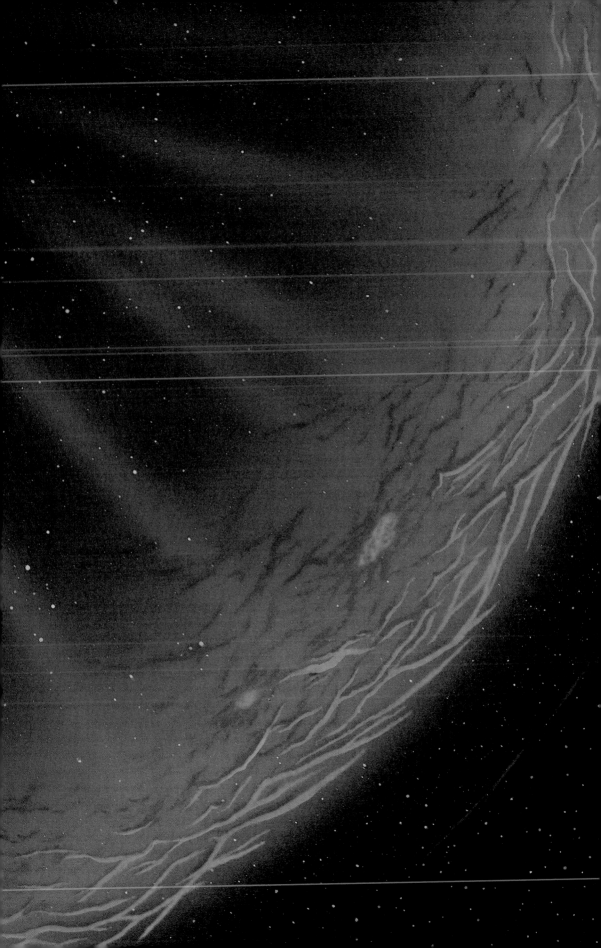

*Spinning through space for millions of years, a protostar builds heat and pressure deep within, creating a core of glowing gases and dust (top). As the nuclear furnace turns on, radiation drives gases away from the forming star. Larger particles able to withstand the heat clump together to form the solid inner planets (middle). In the colder outer regions, planets form of gases and ices. Nine planets circle our sun, with a belt of asteroids separating the inner and outer planets.*

two that orbit Mars. The only planets that are not known to have satellites are Mercury and Venus, the two that are nearest to the sun.

Four other categories complete our inventory of the solar system. The asteroids are small, generally irregular shapes of rock and metal, whose orbits mostly fall between those of Mars and Jupiter. Comets are even smaller bodies of ice mixed with dust and gravel, with long, eccentric orbits that may range nearly halfway to the nearest stars. Then there are grains of interplanetary dust. Smallest of all are the ionized particles of the solar wind, which break free from the solar corona and stream outward through interplanetary space.

Much of our understanding of this little corner of the universe has come to us within the last few decades.

Nicolaus Copernicus and Galileo Galilei, Polish theoretician and Italian observer, were among the first to glimpse the true nature of our solar system. In the three and a half centuries since Galileo's first telescopic investigations, astronomers have employed ever larger and more advanced instruments in their efforts to unveil the secrets of the sun, planets, and satellites that surround us. No observation from the earth's surface, however, is free of the hindering effects of our planet's atmosphere.

Then, within recent memory, mankind finally broke its terrestrial bonds. Powerful rockets carried instruments above the atmosphere to give a new, unimpeded view into space. American astronauts and Soviet unmanned craft brought precious samples of the lunar surface back from the moon. Both the United States and the Soviet Union dispatched exploratory robots to fly out and touch down on the alien surfaces of Venus and Mars, reporting their findings to their human masters by radio and television. Reconnaissance spacecraft were launched by the United States to Mercury, to Jupiter and Saturn, and onward into the vast emptiness of space where they continue to study the environment between and beyond the planets. Names such as *Ranger* and *Voyager* have become as familiar as *Santa Maria* and *Golden Hind*. Not in all previous history has so much been learned about our solar system. It can be explored for the first time only once, and we are experiencing that golden age.

Just as islands in the sea are often born amidst fire and violence, so—we theorize—did our solar system come into being more than four and a half billion years ago. The sun and all of the other major bodies of the solar system were created together, making the earth and its sister planets not the progeny of the sun but rather its siblings.

Before the birth of the solar system, the material that now makes up sun, earth, and even ourselves was dispersed throughout a great cloud of gas and dust that may have extended more than a hundred light-years. The dust grains probably were the "ashes" of many former stars, debris ejected during their death throes. Our cloud might eventually have dissipated and drifted away were it not for a violent and fateful event that took place in nearby interstellar space. A supernova—a truly awesome explosion in which a dying star suddenly becomes a hundred billion times brighter—sent a series of shock waves through the gas cloud. These compressed the debris and triggered the collapse of portions of the cloud to form new stellar systems, including our sun and its planets.

The one small part of the cloud that was to become our solar system quickly contracted under the relentless pull of its own gravity and, as it did, began to spin and flatten to a disk, with the newly forming sun at its center. Because gases become hotter as they are compressed, the proto-sun began to heat up and then to glow. When its interior reached the critical temperature of ten million degrees Celsius, thermonuclear reactions began—and a star was born!

Meanwhile, dust grains in the rotating disk were adhering to one another to create larger particles; these continued to grow until they finally formed the several large bodies we now call the planets. Each of the new planets may have had a disk of debris surrounding it, like a miniature version of the great disk that had created the planets themselves. These smaller rings of material in turn coalesced to become satellites. The entire process, from the collapse of the gas cloud to the formation of the sun, planets, and satel-lites, probably took less than a hundred million years—a blink of the eye compared with the age of the universe.

Not all of the disk material was swept up by the planets. The rock fragments between Mars and Jupiter continue to exist as the asteroids. Those fragments surviving from the outer solar system are made up mostly of ices. Today they are the comets. When comets happen to venture into the inner solar system, heat from the sun vaporizes the ices, blowing the dust out to create the familiar cometary tails. Because they still exist in much the same state as that in which they were formed billions of years ago, asteroids and comets may give us our best clues to the conditions that prevailed at the dawn of the solar system.

The sun is the source of light and the origin of most of the available energy in the solar system; on earth, except in the darkest depths of the sea, every form of life draws its very existence from the sun. A fiery, rotating sphere of gas about 110 times the diameter of earth, the sun develops temperatures that reach approximately 15 million degrees Celsius (27 million Fahrenheit) at its center, but fall off to a mere 5,700°C at the visible surface, the photosphere.

Solar energy is generated near the sun's center by thermonuclear fusion that converts hydrogen to helium—the same process that produces the sudden burst of energy in a hydrogen-bomb explosion. Unlike the man-made bomb, and fortunately for us, the solar nuclear process is both continuous and stable—at least for now and the next few billion years. But this basic stability is hardly reflected in the dramatic activity and errat-ic turbulence seen by solar observers.

The most conspicuous features of the solar photosphere are the dark areas called sunspots, regions in the solar atmosphere that can be as much as 2,000°C cooler than surrounding areas. Sunspots identify regions where strong magnetic fields penetrate the photosphere. Inter-actions between these fields and the solar atmosphere result in a cooling effect that makes the sunspots appear only about a fifth as bright as surrounding regions.

At times the sun produces huge eruptions of glowing gas that can reach

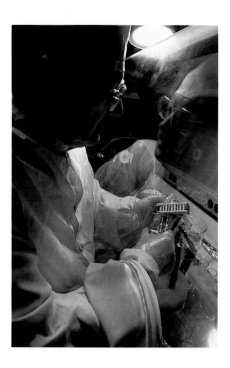

*At the "Lunatic Asylum,"
geophysicist Gerald Wasserburg
prepares components for a new mass
spectrometer, an instrument for dating
samples of lunar rocks, meteorites,
and cosmic dust. "We work like
madmen and date the moon," says
Wasserburg of the name he gave the
ultraclean planetary lab at the
California Institute of Technology.
His research has traced the age of the
solar system back 4.6 billion years,
and fixed its major milestones. At
the University of Arizona, scientists
analyzing the Murchison meteorite
found amino acids representing an
advanced stage of molecular
evolution. In the thin section below,
the dark mineral concentration
contains the amino acids.*

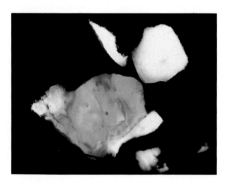

heights nearly equal to the diameter of the sun itself. These spectacular features, called erupting prominences, form along magnetic field lines, especially near sunspot groups. Another violent eruptive phenomenon is the solar flare, a small, intensely brilliant region where matter may be thrown out at speeds up to 600 miles a second. As with erupting prominences, flares tend to be associated with sunspot groups, and the sources of their energy are the solar magnetic fields. But we still do not understand the mechanisms that set them off.

The outermost part of the solar atmosphere is called the corona. It is very extensive and very hot—hotter by millions of degrees than the visible surface. In a sense, the corona really has no upper boundary. Some of its ions and electrons are flung outward to produce the solar wind, a stream of high-energy particles that spread throughout the solar system.

As the particles of the solar wind spiral into the earth's magnetic field, they set off a chain of effects that can be both breathtakingly beautiful and annoyingly intrusive. Intense gusts of the solar wind are responsible for the richly colored displays of the auroras—the northern and southern lights—but they are also a cause of severe short-wave radio interference.

The unpredictable behavior of the sun affects our lives in other ways. Small variations in its luminous energy, if maintained for extended periods of time, can have dramatic effects on our climate, and climatic changes can lead to agricultural crises. Thus there are compelling reasons for learning more about the sun. Since 1973 a series of spaceborne observatories—including Skylab, Helios 1 and 2, and the Solar Maximum Mission—have joined their ground-based counterparts in studying this remarkable energy source.

"Wanderers," the ancient Greeks called the planets. To the casual watcher of the night skies, they are the bright, steady points of light that seem to drift among their stationary, twinkling neighbors. To the astronomer, they are colorful shimmering disks of soft light, often changing their appearance from one night to the next, or from last year to this. But to the planetary scientist who acquires data from distant spacecraft, the planets and their attendant satellites have become real worlds regarded with an intimacy sometimes approaching that felt for the very earth on which we live.

Both the level of our then-existing technical competence and our cultural fascination with the moon and Mars directed our earliest explorations toward the inner region of the solar system. Among its major bodies, the largest is earth and the smallest is the moon; in order of increasing size, the others are Mercury, Mars, and Venus.

Most solid planetary bodies show some evidence of the evolution that followed their formation. Planets with atmospheres reveal the greatest degrees of surface modification from erosion and sedimentation; but flooding by lavas can modify a planetary surface, too.

Neither the moon nor Mercury has an atmosphere, and it is unlikely that either of them ever did. In any event, their respective histories have created a striking resemblance of surfaces: Both are heavily cratered, and both show evidence of extensive volcanic flooding. The similarity between these two bodies stops with the surface, however. Mercury is far denser, indicating that much of its interior is metallic, probably iron.

**M**ars is nearly half again as large as Mercury, with a density that suggests a composition closer to that of the moon. Unlike those bodies, Mars has an atmosphere; although it is very thin—roughly one percent of the density of our own atmosphere—there is evidence that it was much denser in times past. Carbon dioxide in the atmosphere freezes in winter to form dry ice at the poles, where temperatures drop to -125°C (-193°F). Water ice, too, is present in the polar caps, and some of it remains even through the summer.

As we look over the Martian surface, we see the results of what appears to have been widespread water erosion. Great riverbeds and channels, now dry, cut through craters and across plains. Has the water been lost to space, or is it buried in deep permafrost layers beneath the surface, waiting for a warmer climate? We wonder whether liquid water reappears from time to time on the surface of the planet and, if so, whether these warmer periods on Mars are somehow related to earth's long-term climatic changes. Any change in the sun's energy output or passage of the solar system through an interstellar dust cloud should affect both planets simultaneously. To understand the earth's past, we need to know more about the Martian climate.

Another prominent feature of the Martian landscape is the Tharsis region with its four enormous volcanoes. The largest, Olympus Mons, is nearly three times the height of Mount Everest, and so large that it would cover the entire state of Arizona! These volcanoes are probably extinct, but the possibility that they will become active again cannot be ruled out.

The evidence of abundant liquid water on Mars at some time in the past raises the intriguing question of whether life might have gotten a foothold during that wet era. In search of an answer, the United States in 1976 landed two Viking spacecraft on the Martian surface.

Safely placing a vehicle the size of a small automobile on the surface of a distant planet required meticulous planning. Setting the craft down on a rock protruding only a foot or so above the surface could have been fatal to the whole project. I was a member of the landing site selection team, and it was our job to make use of every scrap of available data in choosing sites for the two Viking landers.

As the first one descended to the Martian surface on July 20, 1976, I stood tensely waiting with my friend and colleague Harold Masursky, head of the site team. We were satisfied with the thoroughness of our analysis, and confident that we had chosen a safe location; but as the final moments crept by, we became increasingly nervous. Finally came the shout: Touchdown! All was well.

Immediately the first pictures from the surface of Mars were transmitted back to the control center. The view was both awesome and horrifying—for all around were hundreds of rocks, and contact with any of the larger ones could have destroyed the fragile spacecraft. Hal and I could only stare at one another as our knees turned to rubber.

Each of the two Viking landers carried out several experiments. Some sent back meteorological data; others analyzed the soil. Although the primary goal

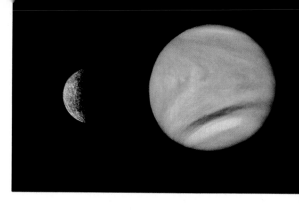

## FACES OF
## THE INNER PLANETS:
## MERCURY TO MARS

*Solid terrestrial planets formed of metals and silicates during the dawn of the solar system. Smallest of the four and closest to the sun, Mercury bakes in blazing heat. Impact craters pockmarking the terrain (below) attest to periods of heavy meteoritic bombardment—episodes that scarred all the terrestrial planets. Lava from ancient volcanoes shaped Mercury's intercrater plains. Venus lies shrouded in a thick atmosphere of carbon dioxide. Trapped radiation creates a hot greenhouse effect and blankets the planet in a continuous, high-altitude windstorm. Earth's distinctive blue appearance derives from its abundant water. Oceans cover almost three-fourths of this*

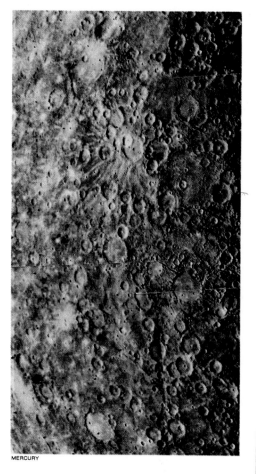

MERCURY

VENUS

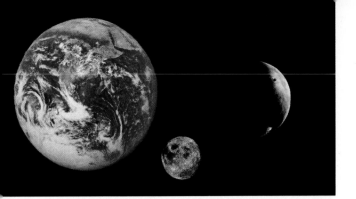

life-sustaining planet, where forces of erosion and shifting tectonic plates slowly reshape the terrain. Clouds of water vapor, like those over East Africa (below), encircle earth in a white veil. On the moon, mountains, craters, and ancient lava flows—the lunar maria or seas—dominate a landscape little changed for three billion years. Mars has the most immense volcanoes in the solar system. Dry channels carving the cratered terrain (below) hint of past flooding; traces of water vapor still moisten the Martian atmosphere. Heavily cratered and irregularly shaped, Mars' two small satellites, Phobos and Deimos, may once have been asteroids.

EARTH, ABOVE; MOON, BELOW

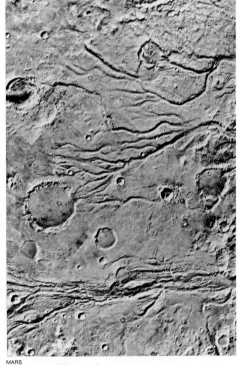

MARS

DEIMOS

PHOBOS

*Forbidding landscape of Venus yields long-held secrets to Venera 13, the Soviet spacecraft that obtained historic panoramas of its rolling hills. Surface temperatures of 460°C (860°F), atmospheric pressure 90 times that on earth, and clouds heavy with sulfuric acid long thwarted robot ground exploration of our closest planetary neighbor. Venera 13, one of several successful Soviet missions to the planet, landed in 1982. The design of the landing gear (sawtooth rim visible below) stabilized the craft both during descent and on the ground. Venera's finds of basaltic rock suggest volcanic activity on Venus, at least in the past. In 1976, Americans set down two Viking landers on the rocky, cratered surface of Mars. The mission's goals: to search for signs of life and to study Martian geology. While monitors aboard Viking have found no indications of life, they have recorded a frosting of water-ice during the winter (below, far right). But Mars' once-abundant liquid water has disappeared, presumably because of long-term climatic changes.*

of the Viking project was to search for evidence of life, no such clues were found; but the results did not provide a clear yes or no answer. Some biologists claim that the experiments were not adequate to detect the entire range of possible life forms; some geologists say that the two landing sites, chosen primarily for safety, were not the best places to look for life. Obviously the chapter on the search for extraterrestrial life in the solar system has yet to be completed.

As Mars is our nearest planetary neighbor outside earth's orbit, Venus is closest on the sunward side. Before the American and Soviet explorations of Venus, very little was known about the planet—primarily because it is perpetually enshrouded by a thick and rather featureless cloud cover. Only images recorded by ultraviolet light show any structure: dusky, low contrast clouds that circle the planet in four days. But where light beams fail, radio waves can often penetrate; so the surface of Venus was mapped by radar, using radio telescopes such as the one at Arecibo, Puerto Rico, with its thousand-foot-wide reflecting dish.

The radar observations showed that the surface of Venus rotated once every 243 earth days—the longest known rotation period of any body in the solar system. This means that the clouds, with their four-day circuit of the planet, are actually skimming over the surface at nearly three times the wind speed of hurricanes on earth.

Since December 1978 an American spacecraft, Pioneer Venus, has used its radar to produce a planetwide topographic map. The results show that most of Venus is quite flat. More than 60 percent of the surface lies within 1,700 feet of the

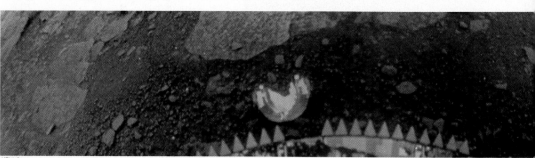

VENUS

mean level; but those few areas where mountains do occur are very high, in some cases rising more than 8 miles, compared with Everest's 5½. Soviet lander vehicles have sent back photographs of the surface showing rocky terrain with surprisingly little evidence of wind erosion.

Like the atmosphere of Mars, that of Venus is composed primarily of carbon dioxide. The clouds that hide the surface from our telescopes are made of droplets of sulfuric acid and possibly sulfur crystals. Because this thick atmosphere traps solar energy like a greenhouse, the surface of Venus is one of the hottest places in the solar system—up to 460°C (860°F) in most places, a temperature high enough to melt lead. Venus, once thought to be a twin to earth and possibly covered with lush vegetation, has turned out to be the closest approximation to hell that we have yet found!

**B**eyond Mars and the belt of asteroids lie the dark, frigid regions of the outer solar system. At such great distances the sun can provide only a feeble illumination and comparatively little warmth.

The remoteness of the outer planets has made them difficult objects for telescopic study, so it is not surprising that our knowledge and understanding of the outer parts of the solar system have been so limited. The first breakthrough came in late 1973 when a planetary probe called Pioneer 10 brought the space age to the outer planets with a flight past Jupiter. Pioneer's was a pathfinder mission, and it paved the way for a more technically advanced craft named Voyager. I was put in charge of the project's television cameras. Between 1979 and 1981, the two Voyager spacecraft encountered both Jupiter and Saturn—and rewrote the textbooks on those two distant planets.

Many of us working on the Voyager project had been involved in the exciting discoveries of the Mariner and Viking missions to Mars, but even that experience had not prepared our imaginations for what we found during the Jupiter and Saturn encounters. While it was clear that much of what we would learn from Voyager would be new, the drama of one extraordinary discovery after another quickly exceeded our expectations.

Jupiter is the largest of the planets, more than 11 times the diameter of the earth. Saturn is nearly as large, and has moreover a magnificent system of rings so extensive they would fill more than two-thirds of the space between earth and the moon. Both planets are encircled by multihued bands of clouds that parallel their equators.

Weather patterns on these giant planets may be quite different from those on earth, Venus, and Mars, because the heat energy that drives the winds comes less from the distant sun than from the great planets' interiors. But there are some similarities. The Great Red Spot on Jupiter, large enough to span several planets the size of earth, is a gigantic anticyclone, or system of rotating winds, corresponding to centers of high pressure in earth's atmosphere but far more violent. High-velocity jet streams have been found in the atmospheres of both Jupiter and Saturn.

Jupiter's satellites—it is known to have at least 16—fall into two groups: those that were created along with the planet itself, and those that arrived later. Most of the former are composed of silicates and ice; *(Continued on page 86)*

MARS

MARS

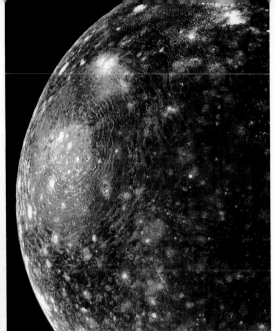

CALLISTO

GANYMEDE

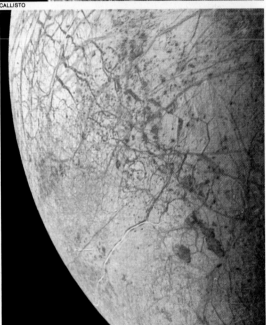

EUROPA

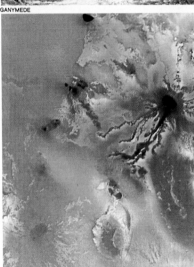

IO

*Jupiter and its four planet-size satellites loom before the peering lenses of Voyager spacecraft. The 1979 flights of Voyager 1 and 2 past Jupiter disclosed a colorfully banded cloud structure with violent whirlpools. In this photomontage, the four largest satellites appear in their relative positions but not in relative scale. Until Voyager, scholars had learned very little about these moons since Galileo first observed them in 1610. Volcanic eruptions rack Io—the only active volcanism known beyond earth.*

*Europa's ice-coated terrain shows dark, ancient cracks. Cratered Callisto may bear more scars from meteorites than any other object in the solar system. Once geologically active, icy Ganymede, says one scientist, presents "a frozen record of tectonics."*

PAGES 82-83: *Mammoth maelstrom, Jupiter's Great Red Spot dominates the southern hemisphere with a perpetual storm system large enough to swallow several planets the size of earth.*

81

# ENCOUNTER WITH
# THE RINGS OF SATURN

*Beautiful and baffling, Saturn's rings grace the heavens of the outer solar system. As the two Voyager spacecraft flew by the planet, their cameras beamed images to earth that astounded scientists at the Jet Propulsion Laboratory in Pasadena, California. Instead of the broad, uniform concentric circles anticipated, there appeared thousands of features—some spiral, some eccentric, with several of the ringlets even kinked or braided. Some of these whirling, icy ring particles "seem to defy the laws of conventional orbital mechanics," says Brad Smith (at right, seated), author of this chapter and head of the Voyager imaging team. With Ed Stone, project scientist for the Voyager missions, Smith manipulates a computer terminal to focus on areas of particular interest within the ring system. In JPL's Space Flight Operations Facility (above), navigators track deep-space probes presently touring the solar system.*

the latter appear to be dark and rocky, and might be captured asteroids. One satellite of Jupiter, named Io, is volcanically active, even more so than earth.

The discovery of huge but inactive volcanoes on Mars had been provocative, creating in many of us a compulsion to find active volcanism somewhere beyond earth. But certainly the outer solar system was where we least expected such activity. I recall vividly the excitement when Voyager found volcanism on that far-off satellite! For me, as for many of my fellow team members, such a moment is the reward for years of planning and patience. It is the very reason that scientists devote so much of their lives to the semi-intelligent robots that serve as extensions of our own eyes and reach billions of miles into space.

Io is still the only body in the solar system, other than earth, known to have active volcanoes. Voyager witnessed nine different eruptive centers on Io, some of them creating plumes that rose nearly 200 miles above the surface.

Included in Saturn's entourage of at least 17 satellites is one that many planetary scientists consider among the most interesting bodies in the entire solar system. It is Titan, Saturn's largest companion—larger, in fact, than the planet Mercury. Titan is the only satellite known to have a substantial atmosphere—mostly nitrogen, but also containing some methane and other organic chemicals.

Titan's atmosphere approximates that of earth several billion years ago, at a time when complex organic chemistry was occurring in earth's atmosphere and oceans. That chemistry eventually led to the formation of life on our planet. This does not mean that we expect to find life on Titan; its surface temperature is -180°C (-292°F), and that is much too cold for the chemical reactions that would be necessary for life to form, much less for its evolution.

But it does mean that Titan's surface may be covered with a layer of very complicated organic sludge, which could well contain many of the molecules that are considered precursors to life. If we could land a Viking-type spacecraft on Titan's surface and perform a chemical analysis, we might learn a great deal about

how life came into being here on earth.

A decade ago, Saturn was the only planet thought to have rings, and theoreticians had a ready explanation. They believed some of the small satellites of Saturn produced gravitational barriers close enough to the planet to keep the ring particles in place.

Then in 1977 Uranus was found to have nine very narrow rings. The theorists hardly had time to respond to this unexpected discovery when Voyager found a ring around Jupiter. It quickly became clear that there is a lot we don't know about planetary rings.

As the first Voyager spacecraft approached Saturn, its satellites, and its rings, it was with the rings that we felt the most relaxed. "The least of the surprises at Saturn will be found within the ring system," I thought. How wrong I was! For the Saturn rings have turned out to be among the most baffling, complex, dynamic systems encountered in all planetary exploration. Irregular dark, spoke-like features that revolve with the ring particles; eccentric rings; rings that have kinks and appear to be interwoven; thousands, perhaps tens of thousands, of individual ringlets: Such revelations have caused many a sleepless night for the Voyager scientists, and more long, wondering nights lie ahead.

Beyond Jupiter and Saturn are Uranus, Neptune, and Pluto. Relatively little is known about these remote planets because of their great distance from earth, and because none of them has yet been visited by a spacecraft. Uranus is surrounded by a set of dark rings and five satellites; Neptune has at least two satellites, and probably three.

Astronomers have searched for rings around Neptune, but so far without success. Vague cloud-like features have been detected in the atmospheres of both Uranus and Neptune. Like Jupiter and Saturn, Neptune has an internal heat source. Curiously, Uranus does not. Uranus is also peculiar in that its axis of rotation is nearly in the plane of its orbit, causing the planet to roll along on its side as it circles the sun.

We know even less about Pluto, the most distant of the planets. Actually, right now Pluto is *not* the most distant. The orbit of Pluto is so eccentric that at

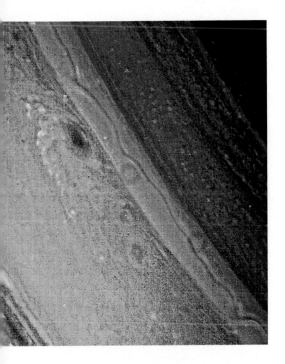

*Belts and zones of Saturn's turbulent atmosphere yield sharp contrast and detail when color-enhanced by a computer. As in the case of Jupiter, cloud-carrying currents of varying speeds form bands around Saturn, their borders often marked by enormous stormlike eddies. Heat welling up from the planet's interior adds its energy to the absorbed sunlight to drive the winds in these currents at more than a thousand miles an hour.*

times the little planet moves inside Neptune's orbit. This happened in 1979, and Pluto will remain closer to the sun than Neptune until the year 1999.

Pluto is smaller than Mercury, and has a satellite about a third its own size. The density of Pluto seems to be very low, as if it were composed almost entirely of ices of various kinds. A thin atmosphere of methane was discovered recently, suggesting that methane ice is one of its major constituents. Pluto seems to have its rotation axis close to its orbital plane, like Uranus. Just why these two planets are "tipped over" is an intriguing question. The composition of Pluto gives it properties we find more characteristic of a comet nucleus than a planet; yet its size surpasses that of typical comets a thousandfold. Perhaps Pluto is some sort of transitional object between comets and planets.

What will happen to the sun and the planets in the eons that lie ahead? If our theory is correct, for a while the evolution of all solar system bodies will continue much as it has in the past. Eventually—approximately five billion years from now—the sun will become unstable. Our once benevolent star will change character, ominously threatening its family as it grows larger, increasing its surface area to radiate away excess energy. Within less than two billion years of the onset of instability, it will become a swollen red giant, engulfing and destroying the planets of the inner solar system and heating and partially eliminating the atmospheres of the outer planets.

After its red-giant phase, the sun will go through a series of pulsations, some violent enough to throw off shells of hot gas. Thus will vanish the remnants of what were once the magnificent giant planets. Still later, as a white dwarf with its thermonuclear energy exhausted, the sun will slowly cool to a dark sphere of carbon and oxygen. Alone, without the planets that accompanied it at birth, it will become an invisible cinder drifting endlessly through space.

The solar system had its origins in the death spasms of unknown stars. In its turn, our sun will give back a share of its own material to space, perhaps to provide the grains of dust from which some future solar system will be born.

# REALM OF
# THE RINGED
# GIANT

*Its successful visit completed, Voyager 2
took a last look at the ringed planet,
whose diameter measures 9 ½ times that
of earth. Beyond the rings, Voyager
brushed past some of Saturn's major
satellites. Hazy, obscured Titan, largest*

of the moons, has the only substantial atmosphere among the satellites of the solar system—high in nitrogen and similar to the earth's early atmosphere. Both Enceladus and Tethys, like Saturn's other smaller moons, appear to be spheres of water ice. Enceladus reflects more light from its frozen surface—in relation to its size—than any other body in the solar system. On Tethys the large impact crater at upper right lies near a huge trench system.

TITAN, ABOVE; ENCELADUS, BELOW

TETHYS

# UPSTAIRS ROOM WITH A CELESTIAL VIEW

From the cage of Palomar Mountain's 200-inch telescope, astronomer James Westphal displays a piece of modern wizardry, the Charge Coupled Device, or CCD. Attached to a telescope, the CCD obtains improved images of objects in space by gathering light more effectively. Nine-ringed Uranus (at far

*right, below) floats with its five moons in the distant night sky. Neptune's best portrait, made with a CCD, shows only major features like the bright ice-crystal clouds high above its northern and southern hemispheres. Pluto appears as a fuzzy speck of light on the fringes of the solar system, orbited so closely by a moon that earthbound astronomers only recently noticed it. To learn more of these remote planets, we must await the findings of spacecraft like Voyager as they push to the outer reaches of the solar system, and the launching of the Space Telescope into orbit above the atmosphere.*

URANUS

NEPTUNE

PLUTO

# OUR CHANGING PLANET EARTH

*By* J. Tuzo Wilson, *Ph.D.*
*Director General,*
*Ontario Science Centre*

From space our water planet presents a view of spectacular beauty. Blue oceans dominate it. The continents and islands, smaller and less conspicuous, appear in patterns of green and brown. Wisps of cloud swirl across the surface, merging toward the poles with the dazzling white of glaciers and frozen oceans. Earth's face seems static, the seas and the continents fixed in their places, all sublimely peaceful.

Yet the continents look like pieces of a jigsaw puzzle, as if they could fit neatly together, or once did. In the last few decades we have come to realize that they did fit together, hundreds of millions of years ago. Far from being fixed in their places, the continents move about.

Earth's beautiful face is cracked; and as the cracks open, the continents move, changing the shapes of oceans, creating mountain ranges, causing earthquakes and volcanoes. Off the coast of Oregon and Washington, one crack has driven a sliver of seafloor crust under the continental edge. The heat generated by the friction of this underthrusting process melts rock; magma wells up, occasionally bursting into the sky—as it has recently at Mount St. Helens.

*Awesome reminder of forces within the earth, a cloud of gas and ash pours from Mount St. Helens, Washington, in July 1980. From this fiery natural laboratory, volcanologists continue to gather information that helps predict eruptions and safeguard human life in regions threatened by volcanic outbursts.*

One and a half miles below the surface of the Pacific, the research submersible Alvin *illuminates a field of pillow lava. Here in the Galapagos Rift, along the edges of the rigid plates that float on the earth's softer interior, magma erupts through deep fissures in the ocean floor. Cold seawater cools the hot lava, which solidifies in distinctive pillow shapes. Narrow ripples of pahoehoe lava (opposite, bottom) show where still-liquid magma washed against older pillow formations. Once the lava hardens, its surface develops cracks such as the yard-wide split (opposite, center) where a sea anemone perches. Water circulating through the fissures penetrates to deeper layers, becomes superheated, and escapes in powerful jet fountains (opposite, top) dense with minerals.*

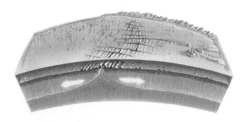

*Changing the face of the globe:
Seafloor spreading takes place
where tectonic plates—giant sections
of earth's outer shell—move away
from each other, as indicated above
by arrows. Magma, molten rock
within the earth, pushes upward
between the edges of the plates to
fill the gap. Cooling and hardening,
the magma becomes new crust.
Scientists have confirmed that such
spreading happens under both the
Atlantic and Pacific Oceans; the
Atlantic widens by $^1/_2$ to 2 inches a
year, the Pacific 2 to 7 inches.*

The gleaming ice sheets are on the move. Are they advancing or receding? What causes ice to shift? Has human activity—air pollution and the carbon dioxide from burning fossil fuels—disrupted nature's pattern of change?

The questions, of vital concern to humankind, challenge scientists around the world. From land and sea and space, the clues pour in. Deep-sea sediments millions of years old and ice that froze in Greenland many thousands of years ago reveal patterns of climates past. The annual growth rings in tree trunks, long a valued tool in archaeological dating, are archives of accurate data for the new science of dendroclimatology—the study of climate by means of tree rings. Its name is not yet in most dictionaries.

Satellites monitor climate on a global scale. Computer models solve complicated equations to simulate climates, test theories of climatic change, assess the impact of variations in the climate system—the atmosphere, oceans, landmasses, and snow and ice cover.

Across the vast stretch of geologic time, the changing array of land and oceans has surely influenced climatic change. And the last few years have brought forth persuasive evidence that astronomical cycles—the slow round of variations in our planet's movement through space—can be matched with the growth and shrinkage of ice age glaciers.

In climatic theory, as in the study of how earth's surface behaves, some of the most adventurous pathways of research were marked out by the German meteorologist Alfred Wegener. Sad to say, his versatile genius did not receive its due until decades after his death in 1930.

Wegener had noted the excellent jigsaw fit of the continents. He had also observed that coal beds, an indication of tropical lushness, lie in cold northern Europe, and that ancient glacial deposits are found in today's tropics. In the fossil records of Europe and North America he found striking similarities among older fossils, but not among younger ones.

To explain these puzzles, Wegener suggested that until about 200 million years ago all land had been concentrated in one supercontinent. Eventually this broke into the present continents, which drifted apart. Continents adrift? What monstrous force could propel them? Physicists knew of none, and they rejected Wegener's proposal. Geologists were equally dubious. In 1926, American geologists condemned the new theory at a major symposium. Since the leaders had spoken out, most people in the United States simply dismissed the idea of continental drift.

The following year I took up the study of geology and geophysics. I attended three major universities—Toronto, Cambridge in England, and Princeton—and if the professors mentioned continental drift at all, they scorned it as a bad joke.

In those days geology concerned itself with labeling rocks, collecting fossils, studying bits and pieces of our planet. One famous physicist compared the subject to stamp collecting.

I had no regrets. I performed my doctoral work not in some cramped laboratory but in the wilderness of Montana's Beartooth Mountains, sleeping under the stars, warmed by a campfire. In the Canadian bush I came to know wild waters and the burdens of portage. I supped on seal meat as a guest of Eskimos, and on fresh moose that I had slaughtered myself. When airplanes came into use, we were resupplied by air and aerial photographs began to guide our explorations. Geologists who had known earlier times thought life was getting soft. But for all our fieldwork, geology was still virtually ignoring the three-fourths of the globe covered by water and ice. The ocean floors? Earth's interior? How would we study them?

Many of us sensed that we would never be able to develop a theory of how the earth's crust behaved until we could study the globe as a whole. To do so, we would have to range the continents and seas to compile mountains of data.

At the end of World War II the tools were at hand, or on the way, and there began a time of revolutionary research that has not yet ended. There were new or improved instruments to measure magnetic and gravitational fields, to trace the flow of heat through the earth, to probe for marine sediments. Radiometric techniques—measuring the decay of radioactive materials—brought new precision to geologic dating. Seismology advanced, and its sound-wave data revealed vast new detail of the architecture of earth's crust.

For the geologist who sought a whole-earth perspective, not the least of the marvels of the early postwar days were the patterns of air travel. Propeller planes flew low and slow; their short range forced them to call at places few of us visit in the jet age. Thus I came to know Iceland and the Azores, Wake Island, the Cocos, and the Seychelles, and I learned firsthand from leading scientists the fruits of their researches in the field. To me, those years were the most exciting the earth sciences have ever known.

One great source of excitement was the confirmation by echo sounding of a globe-girdling mountain range—on the ocean floor! Part of it, the Mid-Atlantic Ridge, was already known; but it now became evident that this greatest of all mountain systems winds more than 40,000 miles around Africa to cross the Indian and Pacific Oceans and end at the Gulf of California. It forms one of two earthquake belts about the earth. The other is the ring of fire around the Pacific rim, with a branch from the Himalayas through the Alps.

Not long after the discovery of the Mid-Ocean Ridge system, the late Harry Hess of Princeton offered a proposal he diffidently called "geopoetry" that synthesized the recent evidence. At the ocean ridges the earth's outer shell, or lithosphere, is split and spread apart by rising currents in the underlying mantle. Lava wells up from the mantle, fills the gap, and becomes welded to the crust on either side. As more lava comes up, adding to the crust, the older rock moves away from the ridge. Confirmation of Hess's theory soon came with the discovery that the pattern of ancient magnetism in the ocean floor can be read, tree-ring fashion, to roughly date the rock. And the dating sequence fits: The age of the rock that forms the ocean floor increases with distance from the ridge crests.

By 1965 many of us were convinced, like Wegener, that the continents were moving—but not, as he thought, independently adrift on the oceans. Today's theory of plate tectonics holds that the continents are *(Continued on page 106)*

## HAWAII: HOW VOLCANOES BUILD ISLANDS

*Shrouded in steam, sizzling lava flows into the sea along Hawaii's east coast during a 1971 eruption of Kilauea's Mauna Ulu vent. The episode extended the shoreline more than 300 yards and created some 75 acres of new land. In such ways lava flows formed the volcanic islands of the Pacific. As molten rock meets the cold water, small streams of lava fracture into particles of black sand. Larger flows harden into lava tubes—solid on the outside but still molten inside—that flow to a resting place on the ocean floor (left and below). When a lava tube begins to crack, it reveals the glow of the molten rock within. After the magma oozes out, it cools along the walls of the crack, creating a larger pillow of lava. Scuba divers photographed these formations at a depth of 40 feet during an October 1972 eruption of Mauna Ulu. Scientists believe that the same process forms pillow lavas during seafloor spreading on the Mid-Ocean Ridge.*

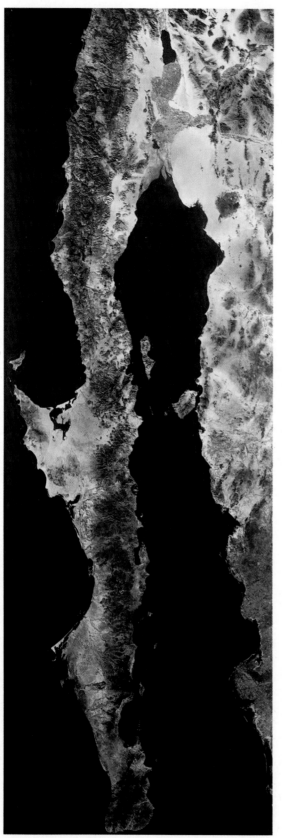

## FROM HIGH ABOVE, EARTH'S FAULTS CLEARLY SHOW

*Mosaic of images from a space satellite forms a portrait of the Gulf of California (left), where the Pacific and American plates adjoin. Millions of years ago tectonic tension split the west coast of present-day Mexico, creating a long leg of land known now as Baja California. Farther north along the plate boundary, traced by the San Andreas Fault system, fractures in the earth's surface (right) run along two edges of California's Mojave Desert— the light-colored area at upper right. The Garlock Fault, extending from the top of the picture, meets the San Andreas Fault at the desert's western corner. Along the coast to the south sprawls the metropolis of Los Angeles.*

PAGES 102-103: *Mineral-rich deposits encrust the edges of pools in this aerial view of Ethiopia's Danakil Depression. Danakil lies in the Afar Triangle where three rift systems converge—the Red Sea, the Gulf of Aden, and a rift valley of East Africa. The depression marks one of the few locations on earth where "seafloor spreading" takes place on land. Scientists consider Danakil and the nearby Red Sea a developing ocean.*

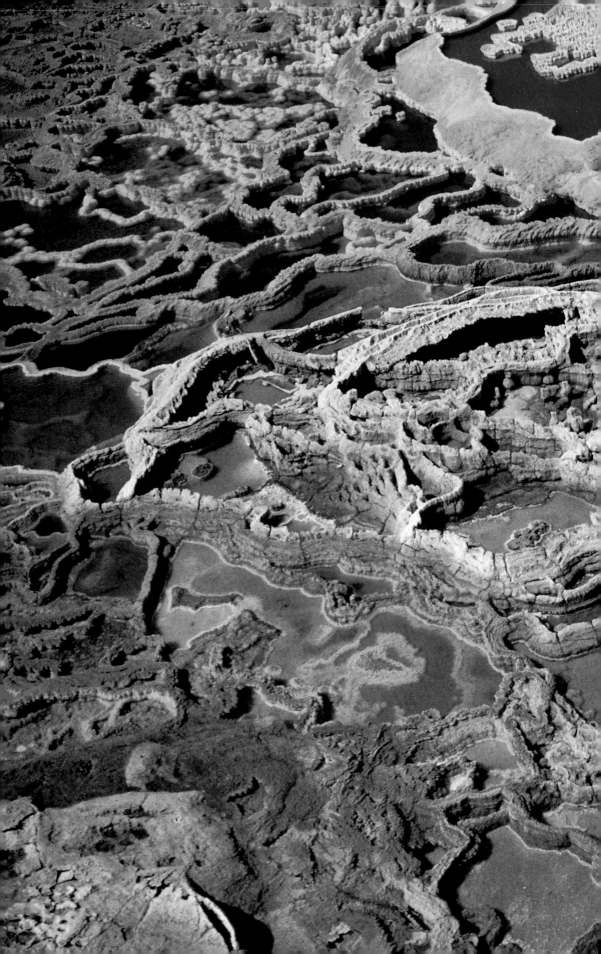

# THE GEYSERS OF CHILE AND ICELAND

*Plume of steam rises from the mouth of a geyser on Chile's Tatio Plateau (left) in the Andes Range. Subsurface water, heated by molten rock, builds up pressure and escapes in a display of the thermal energy that gave the Pacific rim's volcanic chain the name "ring of fire." Below, a geyser in Iceland, along the Mid-Atlantic Ridge, begins its eruption with a giant bubble that pops as steam pressure builds. This one spouts near the original Geysir—Icelandic for "gusher"—that gave its name to the phenomenon.*

embedded like frozen rafts in much larger plates of moving lithosphere. The basaltic ocean plates are younger than the continents, and denser. The continents are much more ancient, more complex aggregations of rock, weatherbeaten and eroded. One scientist has called the continents the "scum of the earth"—with no derogation intended.

Skeptics have wondered how these plates can move, since the earth behaves as a solid to a depth of nearly 2,000 miles. The answer seems to lie in the fact that just under the cold, brittle shell, the earth is very hot, and the heat creates a mobile layer. It is like having a layer of soft butter under the top crust of a loaf of bread. The crust can move.

The movement between the plates can be of three kinds. The plates can move apart, they can converge, or they can slide past one another. The three motions are connected. I can easily visualize them when I open my desk drawer. Inside the desk, as the back of the drawer moves forward, a gap forms. This corresponds to the opening of a fresh ocean floor. The front of the drawer comes toward me, perhaps colliding with the chair or my body. With earth's plates, there is always something in the way, because there is good reason to believe that the planet's size does not change materially. If an ocean is spreading by the creation of new crust, then equal areas of old crust must be absorbed into the interior.

On the floor of the Pacific the Mid-Ocean Ridge is opening at the rate of several inches a year. To the west of the ridge the Pacific plate, one of six large crustal plates, is being pushed northwestward toward the great ocean trenches and the island arcs of the Aleutians, Japan, and eastern Asia.

The evidence suggests that along the trenches and beneath the islands, the rigid surface shell of the earth is being destroyed. The oceanic plate, subjected to intense heat, is evidently bent and forced down into the mantle. These are zones of abundant earthquakes and volcanoes.

Let's go back to my desk drawer for the third kind of plate movement. Along the sides of the drawer, sliding motions occur, without collisions or opening gaps. This does not mean the sliding must be smooth. Think of a very tight drawer.

You may tug and tug without effect, until force overcomes resistance and the drawer slips loose. When a similar slippage happens between plates of the earth's crust, the result is an earthquake.

One area of such shearing begins at the mouth of the Gulf of California. There the spreading motion of the plate boundaries on the seafloor becomes more complicated. The boundaries begin to shear as well as separate, and the Pacific plate slides northwestward relative to the American plate. Because of this shearing, a fragment of western Mexico and California—once attached to the American plate—has broken off and now slides with the Pacific plate. Where the plate boundary runs aground at the San Andreas Fault, the transformation is complete. The shearing action takes over, and the plates scrape past each other.

Off Oregon the process is reversed. Sliding reverts to a spreading motion from ocean ridges. Farther north, the sliding resumes along a fault that extends nearly to Anchorage, Alaska.

Such cracks, where the plate motion is changed or transformed, I have called transform faults. In plate tectonics theory, they are seen as essential parts of the network of plate boundaries. But the concept that great motions can occur at such cracks is comparatively new.

In 1953 two geologists proposed that the part of California west of the San Andreas Fault system had slid northward several hundred miles over the last tens of millions of years. Few believed them. In 1965, when these ideas were still new, I was invited to California to lecture about them. Many were still skeptical. But when I went again in 1982, it was my turn to be astonished. Not only had the idea of large sliding motions in California been accepted, but many in the audience also held that most of Alaska and much of British Columbia consist of fragments carried north by faults that were predecessors of the San Andreas.

There have been other surprises. The concept of seafloor spreading naturally led to investigation of the rifts along the Mid-Ocean Ridge. Research vessels have found the crest quiet in most places. Like movements along faults, activity on the ridge is intermittent. Not until 1977

*Veteran earthquake scientist Charles F. Richter reads the tracings of a seismograph at the California Institute of Technology. The sensitive instrument records vibrations in the ground beneath it. In 1935 Dr. Richter published a numerical scale—still in use and still bearing his name—that enables experts to measure and compare the magnitude of earthquakes.*

did John B. Corliss and John M. Edmond, in the submersible *Alvin,* see great springs jetting warm water from a part of the Mid-Ocean Ridge. They were amazed to observe, as well, totally unexpected forms of life.

"We looked out our ports to see shimmering water streaming up past the submersible with pink fish hovering in the warm water," Corliss said, "white crabs scuttling over the rocks, huge white clams and yellow-brown mussels and long white tube worms with red plumes surrounding the hydrothermal vents."

The jets had a maximum temperature of only about 22°C (72°F); but some two years later off Baja California, the *Alvin* crew found jets roaring like fire hoses at temperatures around 350°C (662°F). They were kept liquid only by the pressure of an almost two-mile depth of seawater. Dark with suspended minerals and dubbed "black smokers," these jets poured out in billows. As they cooled they formed cones and piles of sulfides of iron and other metals. The explorers had discovered an unexpected way in which bodies of ore can be formed.

But surely the most startling discovery of all was the strange realm of life at the jets. Everywhere else on earth, advanced life depends upon the sun for energy and growth. Here were new and extraordinary forms of life, far from sunlight at depths of thousands of feet, thriving in the heated water and dependent for their nutrition upon bacteria and organisms synthesized by the bacteria, through a process in which chemicals rather than sunlight provide the energy to manufacture food.

Among the questions we cannot yet answer are those physicists asked when Wegener set forth his theory of continental drift: What causes the crust to break apart? What drives the plates?

One view holds that heat currents just under the earth's shell stir the mantle and turn it over like water heated in a pan. As the mantle turns, it pulls the overlying shell about. But this idea does not fit well with the observation that the lower mantle behaves as a solid. A second suggestion is that the motion stems from the tendency of surface plates to sink down. This may be part of the story—but only a part. *(Continued on page 116)*

# PLATE TECTONICS: THE SHIFTING PIECES OF EARTH'S SHELL

*Like icebound ships locked in drifting floes, the continents move about the surface of the earth riding huge plates. Where they shove together, they create mountain ranges; where they pull apart, they open oceans. Geologists count six major plates and many smaller ones. Their approximate boundaries appear*

ALASKA    CANADA

MOUNT ST. ELIAS

on the bottom diagram. The reddish
dashed line running along the coast of
North America on the relief map traces
the active edge where the Pacific and
American plates slide haltingly against
each other—except where the irregularly
shaped Juan de Fuca plate (darker shade,
bottom diagram) intervenes. Friction
between the American and Pacific plates
causes strains released sporadically in
earthquakes. The Juan de Fuca plate dips
under the American plate (cutaway view). As
the edge of the smaller plate descends,
some of the rock melts and escapes
through fissures, feeding volcanic eruptions
such as those of Mount St. Helens.

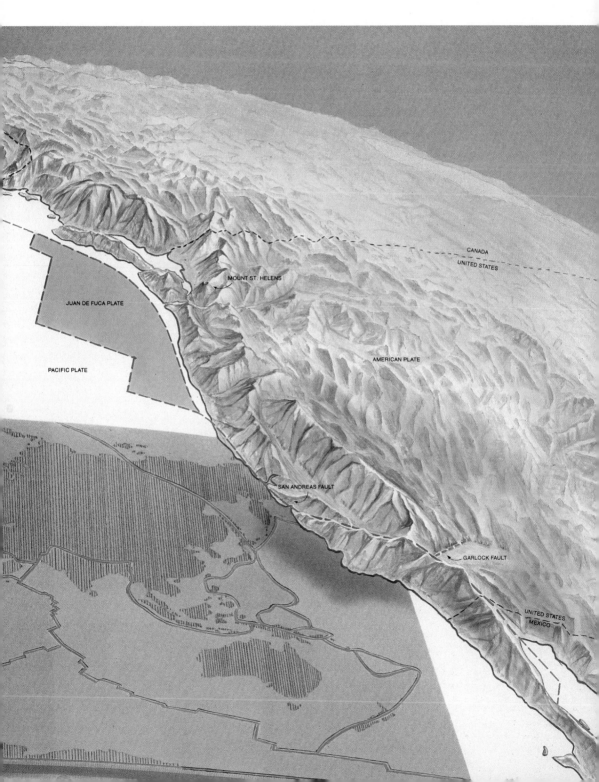

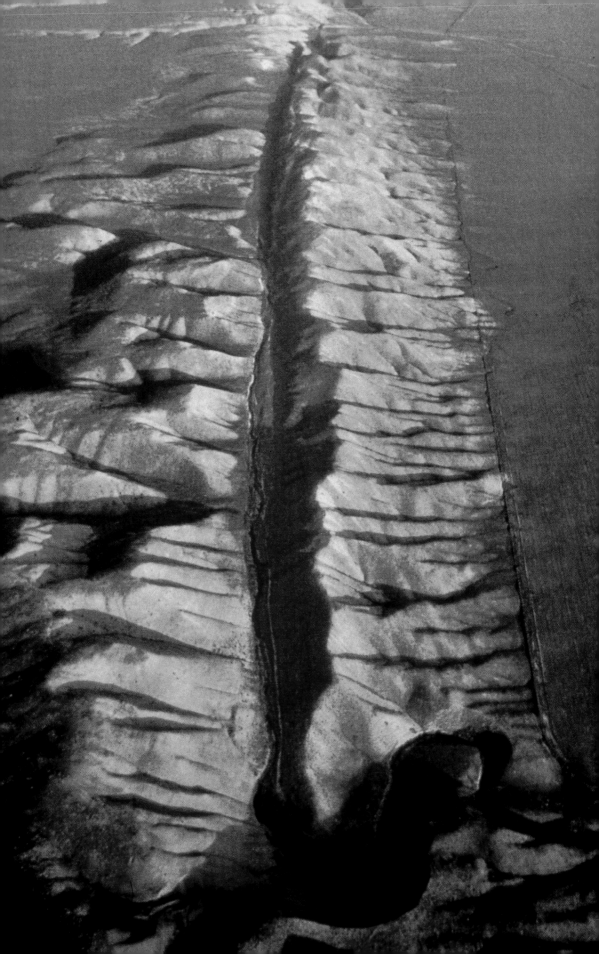

# CALIFORNIA'S COAST DRIFTS NORTHWEST

San Andreas Fault furrows the Carrizo Plain northwest of Los Angeles. Here the Pacific plate slides northwestward past the American plate. Structures built in such active fault zones provide dramatic evidence that not all geologic changes require eons to show their effects. Above, geologist Robert Nason studies a farm fence that crosses the San Andreas Fault near San Juan Bautista, California. Straight and true in 1940, the fence today bends some nine inches out of line. Along another section (above, top left) the shifting earth has stretched the fence, pulling boards loose from their nails. A protractor's scale (above, lower left) measures an offset of five centimeters—some two inches—on a street curb installed about 1940 in the nearby town of Hollister.

*Great lava dome dwarfs two geologists crossing the flat foreground (above) inside the crater of Mount St. Helens. A foot-wide crack in the crater floor reveals rock heated to more than 1,500°F (opposite, above). Rising magma bulges the dome and opens cracks in the dome and crater floor; such activity foreshadows new eruptions. At right, a geologist checks batteries of radios that transmit data every few minutes. His colleagues (far right) aim an infrared radiometer at the lava dome to determine how much heat it gives off.*

## IN THE THROAT OF THE CRATER

# AT THE EDGE OF THE RING OF FIRE

Crown of snowfields and glaciers caps
Mount St. Elias near Icy Bay on
Alaska's southeastern coast. Fossils of
marine animals found in relatively
young rock, which now lies as high as
3,000 feet above sea level, confirm the
rapid uplift that occurs along this
geologically active portion of the Pacific
ring of fire. Opposite, a helicopter rests
on a terrace that abruptly rose more
than 47 feet during an earthquake in
1899. Near here scientists have identified
a "seismic gap"—a zone little touched
by major earthquakes in recent years but
a likely target for one soon. Some 75
seismic stations in southern Alaska
record information that may help
geophysicists to predict the time, place,
and strength of earthquakes. Opposite,
above, a technician on a mountainside
overlooking the Lowe River inspects
a radio-repeater station that relays data
from a seismometer buried about 45
miles away.

Although not everyone agrees, I like to think that "hot spots" may hold the key to the puzzle. Heat generated deep in the earth must escape. This occurs at hot spots, areas in which jets or plumes a few hundred miles in diameter rise through the mantle like heat rising from the Great Plains to form thunderheads. When the heat reaches the surface, it cooks up lava and volcanic eruptions.

It occurred to me that such a stationary hot spot could have created the Hawaiian Islands. In this hypothesis the plume pushes up island-forming lavas. In time the Pacific plate moves off, carrying the island along with it. Eventually the hot spot sends up another island.

The Hawaiian chain runs southeast to northwest, each island progressively older. The island of Hawaii, with its active volcanoes, has been right over the plume. Now another volcanic island seems to be forming 30 miles southeast of Hawaii; still underwater, it may eventually build up to emerge above the surface.

Midway, some 1,500 miles or 2,400 kilometers to the northwest, dates from about 25 million years ago. If the hot spot remained in one place, the Pacific plate has moved at the rate of about a hundred kilometers every million years.

Beyond Midway a chain of seamounts, or underwater islands, continues northwest, ending with one that is 40 million years old. There the chain bends sharply northward. We have identified several other Pacific groups with a parallel pattern.

Worldwide more than a hundred hot spots have been recognized, including the Yellowstone area in the United States and several in East Africa. The pattern that results in plate motion, it seems to me, begins with such hot spots. In East Africa groups of volcanoes have linked up to form rift valleys a few million years old. In Ethiopia a section of one valley connects to the Gulf of Aden and the Red Sea—young, narrow seas opened less than ten million years ago. And they connect with the Indian Ocean, more than a hundred million years old—and growing.

We may have here a picture of the way oceans begin. Hot spots thus may be the prime force in opening oceans and an important mechanism that moves plates.

On the Mid-Atlantic Ridge, hot spots

*Restless dunes tighten their sandy grip on Egypt's oasis of Beshendi in the Sahara, largest desert in the world. Desert encroachment may result from centuries-old patterns of dune movement in rain-poor regions. But in some desert border areas, climatic change and—most likely—human activities have caused neighboring cropland to shrink.*

such as Iceland and Tristan da Cunha seem to have formed before the Atlantic did, for they have left lava trails on each side of the ridge that reach to continental coasts. In other words, these hot spots were pushing up lava while the continents were still together.

In the 1960s I traveled south along Baffin Bay in a freighter canoe with two students and two Eskimo guides. Among moving ice floes at the foot of cliffs we mapped 60-million-year-old lavas of Baffin Island. They matched a similar patch across the bay on the coast of Greenland. To me these are signs of the hot spot that split Greenland from the Canadian Arctic islands and opened Baffin Bay.

Wegener visualized a single splitting up of the continents. Today we think the cycle occurred not once but many times as the oceans opened and closed like concertinas. Before the Atlantic existed, an earlier ocean closed, and North America, Africa, and Europe butted together to form the Appalachians. Much more recently the coasts of once separate India and Asia collided to push up the mighty Himalayas. Is it not strange that oceans give rise to great mountains?

The Mediterranean Sea appears to have been part of an ancient ocean, now much shrunken. Perhaps in time the shores of Africa and Europe will converge to raise mountains. Someday our descendants may ski on the Riviera.

The sunny Riviera seashore transformed into snow-mantled mountains? One of the most exciting aspects of earth sciences today concerns the way in which questions of geology and questions of climatic change seem to overlap.

Solar radiation, of course, supplies the energy for our climate machine. From the sun comes more energy in a week, by one estimate, than we humans have produced throughout our history by burning fuels. At the earth's surface, radiation begins the pattern of atmospheric circulation, which is closely related to the circulation of the oceans.

Ice and snow reflect the sun's rays, thus influencing the amount of heat retained at the surface. Climate is also affected by the fact that water surfaces heat and cool more slowly than do those of the landmasses. The opening of oceans and continental movements would thus have had an important impact on climate across the span of geologic time.

Wegener suggested that an ice age existed 200 million years ago when the continents still lay close together. By a hundred million years ago, the breakup was well under way. Channels opening between continents enabled currents to circulate. Landmasses moving away from the poles could receive equatorial heat. We believe the climate was generally warm, humid, and equable. The picture began to change some 60 million years ago; a general cooling set in. Did plate tectonics trigger it? Plate movements seem consistent with the trend, though scientists look to a variety of causes for climatic change.

The continents continued to drift, opening some seaways while restricting others, particularly the major passage that then existed along the present line of the Himalayan and Alpine ranges.

By ten million years ago, Antarctica was isolated over the pole. Snow fell on the polar continent. The white surface reflected more of the sun's radiation back into space. The present ice sheets began to form; by five million years ago, they were as extensive as they are today.

Between three and four million years ago, the Isthmus of Panama closed, again restricting a seaway. Soon after that came the beginnings of an ice age in the northern hemisphere. By a million years ago the northern ice sheets covered Greenland, much of North America, Scandinavia, and part of Siberia. We have been in a glacial period ever since.

Only very recently have we begun to paint a detailed picture of glacial movement in these last million years. The land has preserved only a sketchy record, for each new advance of the ice obliterated evidence of earlier ones.

In the seas, however, science has struck it rich. We now have the ability to pull long, undisturbed cores from the floors of the deep oceans. Patterns of ancient magnetism and radiometric dating provide a time scale for the record of life contained in the cores. Some of the tiny creatures could live only at certain water temperatures, so the changes in animal life imply changes in temperature.

With mass-spectrometers scientists

Cloud of coral "sawdust" drifts from a drill cutting a core from a living coral head (opposite) in the Gulf of Mexico. At right, one of the divers removes a portion of a core from the diamond-tipped barrel. Corals deposit annual bands somewhat resembling tree rings. Variations in the bands indicate changes in water quality and temperature; extreme cold causes the coral to form an extra band between annual rings. Off Florida, a single core from a ten-foot-high coral head showed a continuous record of weather changes as far back as the early 1600s. Above, divers carry a hydraulic drill across the coral-strewn floor of the South China Sea off the Philippines. Drilling does not kill the coral colony; divers insert a concrete plug into the hole, and within a year the coral has started to grow over the plug.

examine the two forms, or isotopes, of oxygen that exist in varying proportions in the minuscule fossil shells. One of these isotopes, oxygen 18, increases in ocean water—and thus in the shells—as the amount of ice and snow increases on the planet.

The new evidence was gathered and analyzed in a major research project called CLIMAP, begun in the 1970s and sponsored by the United States. CLIMAP (short for Climate: Long-Range Investigation, Mapping, and Prediction) produced data for maps depicting past climatic and geographical conditions. They showed not only glaciers but also areas of desert, forest, and grassland.

The material acquired thus far shows that the earth has generally been cold during the last million years, but the climate has swung through a succession of glacial and interglacial stages. We now know of about a dozen major cycles of ice advance and retreat, and they recur every hundred thousand years.

For CLIMAP scientists on the frontiers of research, the drama is not merely in the detailed re-creation of ice age history. In 1976 these scholars reported that the climate cycles observed in deep-sea core data provide support for a theory of what caused the ice sheets to grow and recede. Wegener himself wrote a book suggesting the theory, elaborated some 40 years ago by the Yugoslavian scientist Milutin Milankovitch. It holds that ice age fluctuations are caused by changes in the earth's movements in relation to the sun. These changes occur in three distinct astronomical cycles. Milankovitch tried to show how the cycles might combine to control the seasonal and geographical distribution of solar radiation reaching the earth—and hence the general temperature.

One of the cycles is the slow change in the earth's orbit around the sun—from a circular path to a slightly elliptical one and back again. It takes about a hundred thousand years to complete this pattern.

A second cycle involves changes in the earth's tilt, which affects our seasons. The third cycle of change is our planet's wobble about its axis—a movement somewhat like that of a toy top as it runs out of spin.

With a distribution of lands around

*Thrusting a wire-mesh basket into a stream, a geologist collects samples of sediment from the runoff of Hilda Glacier high in the Rocky Mountains of Alberta. Over the last two centuries this receding field of ice has left abundant evidence of its former extent. Through the study of such alpine glaciers—those formed on summits or in valleys—scientists seek clues to the advance and retreat of the continental glaciers, the massive ice sheets that covered much of the earth thousands of years ago.*

the poles similar to the present one, all three astronomical cycles would theoretically produce seasonal trends resulting in the growth or decline of the ice sheets. CLIMAP researchers compared the timing of the Milankovitch cycles with the fluctuations evidenced by the deep-sea cores. The two sets matched.

According to the Milankovitch theory, the combination of the three astronomical cycles moved the earth from a full ice age 18,000 years ago to a climatic optimum about 6,000 years ago. Then the downturn began; and for the next several thousand years the Milankovitch hypothesis forecasts cold, with increasing ice.

Does the record of the most recent past bear this out? For the last 10,000 years, archaeology and written history enrich our picture of the climate. Not only ocean sediments but also pollen grains in bogs and lake bottoms provide details of these more recent millennia.

Tree rings, notably of those long-lived patriarchs of the West, the bristlecone pines, show their own patterns of growth all the way back to 6276 B.C. From tree-ring analysis scientists have created climate maps for each year back to 1600.

Ice cores lock in a continuous record of atmospheric changes. Drilling to bedrock in Greenland, scientists tapped layers of ice believed to be nearly 100,000 years old. Dust of volcanic explosions is frozen in the layers. Matched against history's accounts of volcanic eruption over the last 900 years, the dust in the time scale of ice cores varied by no more than a year.

It was Alfred Wegener who pioneered in weather research on Greenland's ice sheet, establishing the first observation station there. He was a kindly leader. In 1930, after he had left two men to winter over, he decided to make one last trip to assure their supply of food and fuel. On the return journey, he died, the cause unknown. He was buried in the snow by a companion, who used the great man's skis as his grave marker.

Combined results of the studies of the recent past show that 10,000 years ago the ice sheets over northern Europe and North America had begun to retreat. The earth continued to warm up until 6,000 years ago. Since then the average temperature has slowly and irregularly dropped, with a particularly cold spell about 2,800 years ago and another about 500 years ago. Around that latter date began the four cold centuries known in European history as the Little Ice Age.

One of the harshest years of those centuries was 1816—the "Year Without a Summer," when New England recorded summer frost, crop failures, and local famine. It came on the heels of three noteworthy volcanic explosions: Soufrière on the West Indies island of St. Vincent in 1812; Mount Mayon in the Philippines in 1814; and Tambora in Indonesia in 1815, which flung out some 30 cubic miles of ash in one of the greatest eruptions in history.

Volcanic ash in the atmosphere reflects solar heat back into space, but allows heat radiated from earth to pass freely. Thus ash tends to cool the planet; but the chill seems to be temporary.

After the Little Ice Age ended more than a century ago, a widespread warming trend developed, building to a maximum around 1940. Since that time the northern hemisphere has shown a slight cooling trend. From our research into climatic cycles we should expect more cold, an icy future. But new factors cloud the picture.

Since the Industrial Revolution began, the burning of coal, oil, and gas has released increasing amounts of carbon dioxide into the atmosphere. It produces exactly the opposite effect of volcanic ash. Carbon dioxide lets solar heat through to the earth and keeps the earth's radiant heat in—just as the glass shell of a greenhouse does. This greenhouse effect tends to warm the earth.

At the same time, human activity has thrown particles of dust and smoke into the atmosphere. These veil the planet in the same manner as volcanic ash—producing a cooling effect.

Which of these factors will predominate? I believe the weight of scientific opinion is betting on the greenhouse effect. So long as humankind consumes fossil fuels at the present rate, our planet is likely to get warmer. But no one can be certain. The code in which the secret of climatic change is written has not yet been fully deciphered.

# ICE
# CORING
# AT
# 17,000
# FEET

*Scientists and porters climb toward the Great Ice Plateau in the Zanskar Range of the Himalayas. On the plateau they extract cores of ice using a hand-turned drill with a hollow bit. The chore proves exhausting in the oxygen-poor air more than 17,000 feet above sea level. At far left, an aluminum ice saw slices off a three-inch length from an ice core. Scientists wear plastic suits to protect the sample from contamination—even a drop of sweat could render later findings invalid. At left, a team member weighs an ice section. In their laboratory at the University of New Hampshire, the glaciologists will analyze this and more than 1,500 other samples they collected. Tests will include measuring dust, salt, and other faint traces in the melted ice. From this information, the scientists can reconstruct not only the climatic patterns, but also the movement of air masses over the Indian subcontinent for the last 30 years.*

# PROBING THE NEW BIOLOGY

*By* RICHARD F. THOMPSON, *Ph.D.*
*Professor of Psychology and Human Biology,*
*Stanford University*

Many years ago when I was a young member of the faculty at the University of Oregon Medical School, my baby daughter and I were strolling near our home in Beaverton and came upon a large garter snake. As the snake moved away, she pointed to it and said "bow-wow." She was just learning to talk, and the animal she knew best was our dog. For a two-year-old, though, she was not a bad biologist. She had succeeded in classifying the snake as a living thing, as an animal, and even as a vertebrate.

Most of us are so used to the variety of life around us that we take it for granted. Much of this knowledge is very old. Our early ancestors probably knew more about the life forms they dealt with than we do about those that surround us today. Every "primitive" tribe in the world has its own pharmacopoeia—including knowledge of a large selection of plants that can help in curing ailments or in hurrying an enemy into the next world.

For a very long time the field of biology was primarily concerned with describing and classifying plants and animals. At the turn of the century, with the confirmation of Gregor Mendel's classic studies of 35 years earlier, biologists entered another stage, one that emphasized the investigation of the mechanisms of heredity. And since 1953, when James Watson and *(Continued on page 130)*

*Harboring the secret of life, DNA— deoxyribonucleic acid—stores the genetic blueprints for all living things. Discovery of DNA's double-helix structure, shown in this computer image, launched the age of the new biology.*

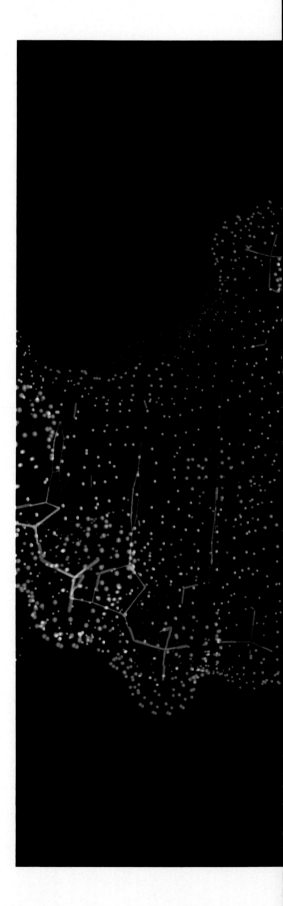

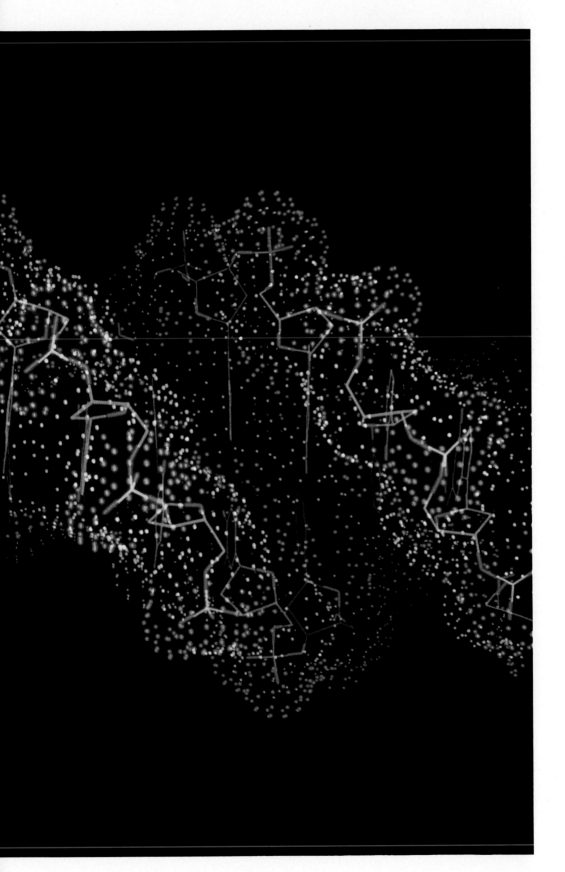

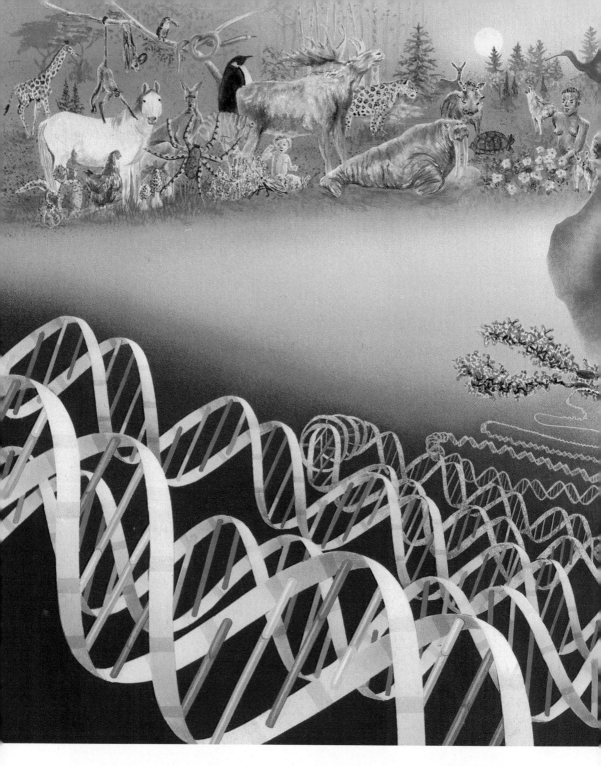

## DNA: CARRIER OF THE GENETIC CODE

*DNA exists within each chromosome inside every cell of every organism from lowly amoeba to human being. Its double helix, or spiral-ladder structure, appears deceptively simple. Alternating sugars and phosphates comprise its two sides, and pairs of molecules (adenine and thymine, guanine and cytosine)*

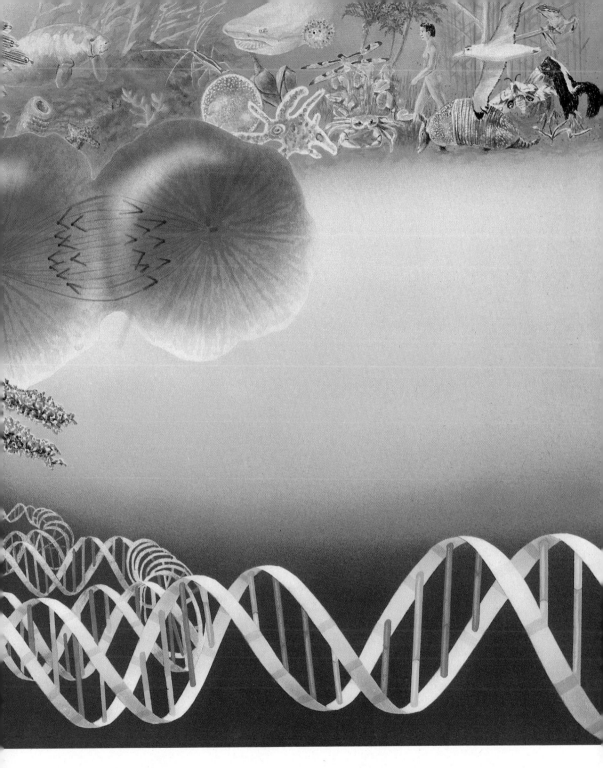

form its rungs. Their varying sequence along the ladder determines the genetic message—to create a moose or a spruce, to scent a hyacinth or give a baby curly hair. Each molecule of DNA consists of coded segments, or genes, that carry hereditary instructions for making the proteins that govern all life processes. When a plant cell or an animal cell prepares to divide, the loosely arranged DNA chain replicates, then condenses into tightly coiled chromosomes (center of painting). As one cell splits into two, twin sets of chromosomes, each tugged into a V shape, migrate along specialized fibers.

## IN SEARCH OF LIFE'S BEGINNINGS

*When bacteria ruled the world—for more than half of earth's nearly 4.6-billion-year history—they left behind evidence that may point to the origins of life. At a site in Western Australia, scientists discuss a well-preserved stromatolite —the inorganic debris built up by an ancient bacterial community. At right, top, wavy layers formed between*

*sheets of bacteria pattern a stromatolite from the site. A microfossil found in rocks nearby (right, center)—dated at 3.5 billion years—may prove one of the oldest examples of organisms yet found. Earlier work at Gunflint in Ontario uncovered bacterial microfossils about two billion years old (bottom)—sparking new quests for traces of first life.*

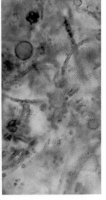

Francis Crick worked out the structure of the genetic material—deoxyribonucleic acid, or DNA—in chromosomes, a "new biology" has given us a much more profound understanding of life.

When you stop to think about it, the diversity of living things is almost unbelievable. Over the centuries, scientists have managed to classify more than a million species of animals and half a million of plants. As many as ten million species may still be undescribed.

Our own class, mammals, has a modest total of about 4,500 living species. Insects, on the other hand, account for more than 750,000. A woman once asked the late J.B.S. Haldane, the famous British biologist, if he knew much about God. Haldane replied that he did not, but that he did know that God must be exceedingly fond of beetles. Of all the animal species we know, three-fourths are insects, and fully a third of the insects are beetles.

Sometimes it has proved difficult to determine whether an organism is a plant or an animal—or neither. The viruses are a particular puzzle. They cause a wide range of diseases in humans, from the common cold to poliomyelitis and probably a few forms of cancer. Some biologists do not even think they should be considered as living things. Each virus contains a bit of genetic material surrounded by a protein coat. Alone, a virus cannot reproduce; it must invade a host cell and make use of its internal parts.

Viruses aside, all living species demonstrate a remarkable unity in their basic functional element, the cell. Donald Kennedy, an eminent neurobiologist who is now president of Stanford University, offers a favorite example of the diversity and unity of life in his introductory biology lecture to Stanford sophomores. Consider the spruce and the moose. They are both living creatures—but how different! One is a plant that grows more than a hundred feet tall, never moves from its place of birth, and manufactures its food from sunlight and carbon dioxide. The moose, though it is one of the larger animals, is dwarfed by the spruce. The moose moves about, obtains its food by eating plants, and leads a complex social life. It is hard to imagine two more different examples of living things.

Yet if we were to take a tiny bit of tissue from each and examine it under a microscope, these two creatures would suddenly appear much more alike. Both are made up of tiny cells, and these cells look very similar, except for their surrounding layers. The tree's cells have hard walls, the moose's have flexible membranes; but all the cells are discrete units. Each cell has several kinds of organelles—little organs enclosed in their own membranes. One of these organelles is the cell nucleus, a central region that contains the chromosomes, the repositories of heredity.

In contrast to the typical animal and plant cells are the bacteria—more than 5,000 species of them. All bacteria are single, primitive cells without nuclei or other organelles. Cells of this rudimentary type are called procaryotic ("prenucleus") cells, and they are much more ancient than the cells with a nucleus. Although there are not so very many species of these organisms, their numbers are immense. A single ounce of good, fertile soil can contain as many as ten billion individuals.

Many single-celled animals, such as the amoeba, and all multicelled plants and animals alive today are made up of the kinds of cells that contain a nucleus and other organelles. These are called eucaryotic ("true nucleus") cells. As we have said, the spruce and the moose are composed of cells that look very much alike, although they can be distinguished in the microscope. Furthermore, if we go into the biochemist's laboratory and compare the chromosomes within the cells' nuclei, we find them remarkably similar: Packed within each chromosome is a long chain of the chemical DNA. But in one vital way, the chromosomes of the two species are very different. Each has its own distribution of thousands of genes—tiny bits of the DNA—and these genes determine distinctive hereditary characteristics.

We can abandon the spruce and the moose and compare other species, as alike or unlike as we wish. The results always lead back to the same conclusion: The commonality of the genetic code in the DNA indicates that all forms of life that exist in the world today—bacteria, plants, animals, you and I—are descended from the single type of organism that proved best suited to survive the rigors of our early planet.

How these organisms actually began is still unknown. Our certain knowledge goes back only as far as fossil records of very ancient bacteria. The synopsis that follows is our best guess:

After the oceans formed, they gradually filled with a vast array of molecules—the "prebiotic soup" of the early planet. These molecules continuously formed various combinations, and presumably several of these developed the ability to replicate, or make copies of themselves. The key to life in any sustained sense, of course, is the ability to reproduce. But apparently only one of these combinations survived the extreme environmental conditions during the millions of years of the earth's early history: DNA, or perhaps a similar forerunner.

The earth began to form about 4.6 billion years ago. The first life probably appeared as single-celled bacteria little more than a billion years later. One of the greatest changes in earth's history began perhaps 2.7 billion years ago. Certain bacteria similar to algae developed the ability to produce oxygen by utilizing carbon dioxide and extracting energy from sunlight. At that time the earth's atmosphere had almost no free oxygen. These new organisms were responsible for greatly increasing the free oxygen in the atmosphere.

Then, approximately a billion years ago, oxygen-consuming eucaryotic cells evolved, each with its well-developed nucleus containing DNA and with several other internal structures as well.

Among the most remarkable of these other organelles are the mitochondria. Often shaped like tiny kidney beans, they have a vital function: to produce energy for the cell.

The internal structure of the mitochondria is complex. These organelles, in fact, have a life of their own. When a cell divides, each new cell inherits some mitochondria from the parent cell. At this rate they would soon be used up in cell division as a new animal grows, but the mitochondria themselves divide to form new mitochondria within the new cell. Each mitochondrion has its own DNA,

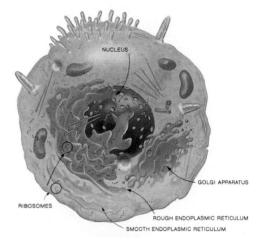

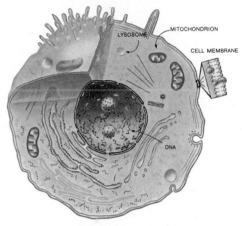

*New biology revolves around study of the delicate systems within cells. A three-dimensional view and a partial cross section of a typical animal cell show internal structures called organelles. The nucleus stores loose chromosomal strands containing the genetic material DNA, which provides for replication and protein manufacture. Amino acids link together at the ribosomes, to form life-sustaining proteins. Proteins travel through the rough and smooth endoplasmic reticula; many go through the Golgi apparatus for further processing. Digestion occurs in the sac-like lysosomes, and mitochondria produce the cell's energy. The cell membrane, composed of protein and fat, controls passage of the various molecules entering and leaving the cell.*

# FROM SINGLE CELL TO COMPLEX INDIVIDUAL

*Miracle of life unfolds in the growth of a sea urchin from a single cell—the simple beginning shared by all living things. Photographs below document the three-week development from fertilized egg to late larva. Of many sperm (left inset), only one will penetrate to fertilize the egg, which then begins to divide. During mitosis, or division, each cell's*

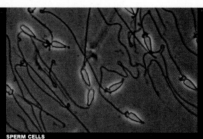

SPERM CELLS

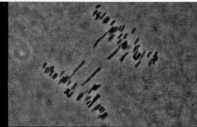

CHROMOSOMES DURING CELL DIVISION

FERTILIZED EGG

FIRST DIVISION

4-CELL STAGE

32-CELL STAGE

BLASTULA

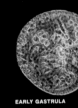

EARLY GASTRULA

PRISM STAGE

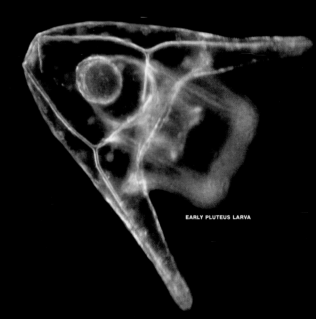

EARLY PLUTEUS LARVA

*chromosomes double and then separate (right inset), passing on identical genes to the two newly formed cells. By the 32-cell stage, a mysterious change occurs. Cells begin to specialize, and they further differentiate in the blastula. A gut starts to indent in the early gastrula. The prism-stage embryo has skeletal rods that extend to support arms in the early pluteus stage. A fully developed gut enables the pluteus to feed on plankton. Below, the future adult grows within the late pluteus larva. Through study of such development, scientists hope to solve one of life's enigmas: How does a single cell give rise to the many tissues and organs that constitute, for instance, a human being?*

enabling it to reproduce independently of the nucleus.

Intriguingly, the mitochondrion resembles a procaryotic bacterial cell. It has DNA but no nucleus. Many biologists now think that the ancestors of mitochondria were free bacteria that were ingested by other cells and became very specialized parasites, or rather symbionts. The relationship between a cell and its mito-

mal way. When this trait for abnormal hemoglobin is inherited from only one parent, it has little or no adverse effect on the person's health; indeed, it provides resistance to malaria. But this special adaptation on nature's part has a negative aspect; for if the mutated gene is inherited from both parents, the result is an often fatal disease called sickle-cell anemia, characterized by a distinctive crescent-

*Adult sea urchin remains a laboratory favorite for scientists studying how embryos grow and cells specialize. Like all higher organisms, the sea urchin reproduces sexually, an evolutionary advance that ensures individual diversity within species. Sperm and egg each supply an offspring with half of its genetic makeup. In contrast, scientists can artificially halt diversity in its tracks by creating clones—genetically identical individuals—produced asexually. Clones of zebra fish embryos (below) prove valuable in genetic research.*

the two components with a different radioactive material. After the treated viruses invaded the bacteria and multiplied, the researchers found that many of the new viruses contained labeled DNA, but none had labeled protein. The demonstration clearly confirmed that the agent of heredity was DNA, not protein.

DNA was first isolated in 1869 by a German chemist. He extracted the colorless, slightly acidic substance from the nuclei of cells and named it nucleic acid. The specific chemical composition of DNA was known by the early 20th century; but in the early 1950s no one yet understood its physical structure, and therefore how it coded and transmitted the information of heredity. Scientists began the race to answer these questions.

In 1951 James Watson, a young American scientist, arrived in England to study molecular structures at Cambridge. There he met Francis Crick, a British physicist, and the two unknown researchers set about to determine the three-dimensional structure of DNA.

They succeeded dramatically in 1953. Surprisingly, perhaps, they did not actually conduct any laboratory experiments. Instead, they collected all the available evidence and tried to build plausible molecular models of DNA using small metal models of the component molecules and much hard thought. Critical information came from X-ray diffraction photographs of DNA taken by Maurice Wilkins and Rosalind Franklin at King's College, London. From indirect evidence and painstaking deduction—and after nearly two years of trial and error—they developed the famed "double helix" model.

DNA's chemical composition, analyzed decades after its discovery, is quite simple. It consists of four types of molecules called nucleotides. Each is made up of a sugar-phosphate group and a nitrogenous compound called a nucleotide base. The four bases are the molecules adenine (A), guanine (G), thymine (T), and cytosine (C). DNA is simply a long sequence of these four nucleotides.

But as Watson and Crick determined, the *structure* of DNA—how the four molecules are hooked together, over and over—allows for almost infinite variety. The twin strands of a DNA chain

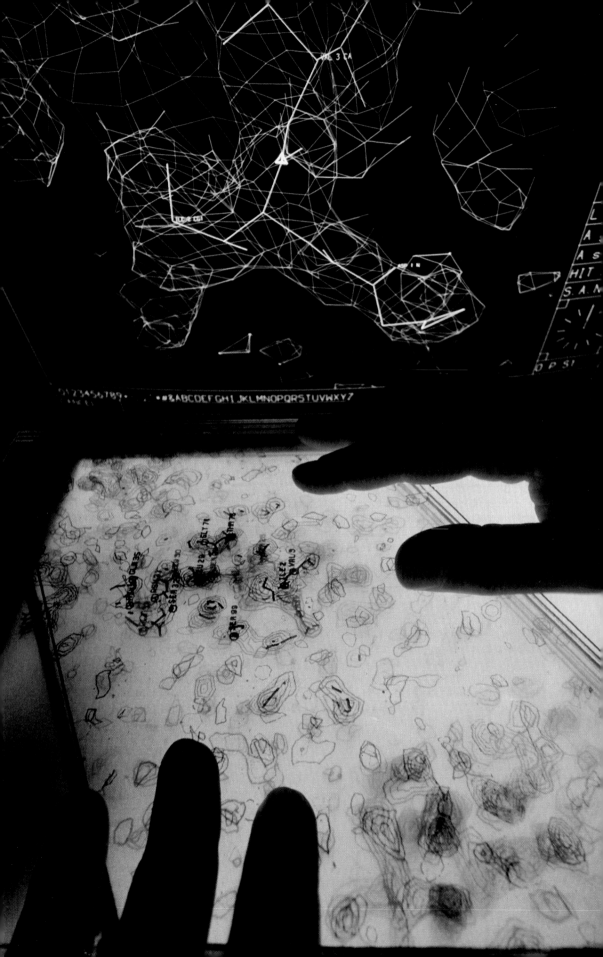

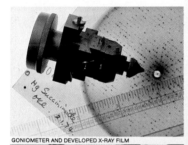

GONIOMETER AND DEVELOPED X-RAY FILM

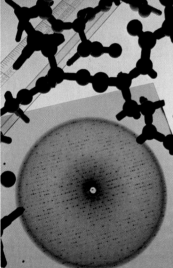

MOLECULAR MODEL AND X-RAY FILM

DIFFRACTOMETER, WITH GONIOMETER

*To visualize the shape of things unseen, scientists create a three-dimensional picture of molecules in detail that even an electron microscope cannot provide. The technique, known as X-ray diffraction, goes beyond chemical composition to reveal a molecule's physical structure. Above at right, at the National Institutes of Health, biochemist Gary Gilliland prepares to make an image of a molecule. He positions a crystallized enzyme in the goniometer of a diffractometer for X-ray bombardment. The goniometer holds the crystal in a thin glass tube; developed film reveals the X-ray diffraction pattern of the enzyme. The results (opposite): A computer-drawn molecular model and an electron density map. From a molecule composed of thousands of atoms, these models show the area occupied by only a few hundred. Solving the structure of an entire molecule may take several years. Interpretations of the maps can yield a physical model; a segment of one zigzags above the X-ray film (above, left). Knowing a molecule's structure provides a key to its function. Researchers even now try to design new wonder drugs from computer models.*

137

wrap around each other to form a double helix. The two strands are bonded together by hydrogen atoms. The DNA chain thus resembles a spiral ladder. The nucleotides on a given side can occur in any order, for example, AGCTCCATG; but that order then determines the order of molecules on the opposite side. A will bond only with T, and G bonds only with C. When the chain is split apart during cell division, an enzyme positions available nucleotides to form a new and complementary "partner" for each strand, thus replicating the double helix.

As Watson explains, "Before the answer was known, there had always been the mild fear that it would turn out to be dull, and reveal nothing about how genes replicate and function. Fortunately, however, the answer was immensely exciting. The structure appeared to be two intertwined strands of complementary structures, suggesting that one strand serves as the specific surface *(template)* upon which the other strand is made. If this hypothesis were true (which it is now known to be!), then the fundamental problem of gene replication, about which the geneticists had puzzled for so many years, was, in fact, solved."

It is the varied sequence of the four molecules in DNA that provides its coded "information." That understanding gives us a more precise way of defining a gene. It is a minute section of DNA that codes for a specific protein.

If all the DNA in a single human cell were to be unraveled as a single thread, it would be about two yards long, and would contain information equivalent to 600,000 printed pages—a library of at least two thousand books!

Once the structure of the DNA molecule was known, progress in understanding how genes work and how proteins are made was very rapid.

As we have seen, a protein is a complex sequence of amino-acid molecules. The same year that Watson and Crick explained DNA, Frederick Sanger, also at Cambridge, first determined the complete amino-acid sequence of a protein—insulin. This stimulated a wave of research on the protein-making process.

Our bodily tissues and organs are made up of several thousand kinds of proteins. All the coded information that

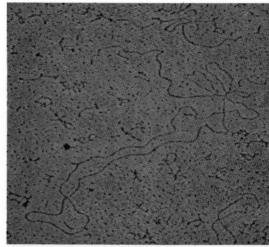

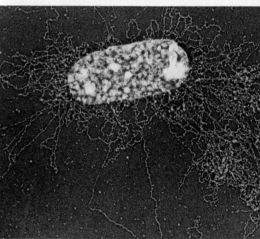

*Magnified thousands of times, a tangled web of DNA unravels outside a capsule-shaped bacterial cell*—Escherichia coli—*disrupted to allow its DNA to spill out. Each human cell contains chains of DNA totaling about six feet—much more than the* E. coli *cell. The discovery that enzymes "edit" DNA's genetic message before the cell can begin making protein intrigues biologists. At top, loops of DNA indicate areas of seemingly unused genetic information. Some scientists speculate that this excess DNA may help regulate protein production.*

is needed to manufacture these thousands of proteins is stored in the DNA molecule—that is, the information to set the sequence of amino acids that will determine the kind of protein, whether insulin or, say, hemoglobin. The actual work of deciphering the DNA code and assembling the proteins is done largely by another substance in the cell called RNA, or ribonucleic acid.

Twenty different amino acids are used in protein production. Although DNA consists of only four nucleotides, it must code for all 20 of the amino acids in order to produce the body's full range of proteins. It does this by using a sequence of three nucleotides to code for a given amino acid.

**S**olving DNA's coding system has led us to a promising new field, that of genetic engineering.

The concept of genetic engineering is quite simple, although the mechanics are rather involved. The genetic code to produce a particular protein is incorporated into the DNA of selected bacteria. The bacteria then reproduce manyfold more bacteria that have the new gene. All these bacteria can manufacture the desired substance.

In other words, bacteria can now be harnessed and modified to produce a desired protein such as insulin or interferon, which so far cannot be synthesized in test tubes but only made by living organisms. Meanwhile the goals of genetic engineering have rapidly broadened, and range from assuring an abundant source of a needed medicine to creating organisms capable of ingesting petroleum and thus coping with oil spills.

The genetic-engineering technique of "cutting" DNA employs a chemical called a restriction enzyme. Bacteria apparently developed such enzymes to protect themselves from invading viruses; by severing the DNA, the bacteria could neutralize or restrict the virus. More than 350 restriction enzymes have now been identified. Each literally cuts the DNA, and always at the same place or places unique to that enzyme. Molecular biologists can use a selection of these enzymes to carve up DNA into specified pieces. Conveniently, these pieces frequently have "sticky" ends that readily recombine—an advantage when they are inserted into other pieces of DNA.

At Stanford and the University of California at San Francisco, scientists found that they could cut open a plasmid—a small, closed loop of bacterial DNA—with a restriction enzyme. After the plasmid is cut, foreign DNA is inserted and attaches at the sticky ends. The succeeding generations of bacteria carry the new, modified plasmids, which enable the bacteria to produce the kind of protein desired by the researchers. DNA from different organisms, including humans, can be combined to form new DNA—"recombinant DNA."

The species of bacteria favored for genetic engineering is *Escherichia coli,* commonly shortened to *E. coli.* It offers a number of advantages, the greatest being that we know more about its genetic makeup than we do of any other organism, because it has been studied for such a long time. *E. coli* normally lives in the intestines of humans. It is not an "infection," but instead a necessary element for proper digestion of food, and it manufactures vitamin K. Here is another example of symbiosis: We provide a home for *E. coli,* and in return it helps us maintain proper nutrition.

A much simpler molecule than insulin is somatostatin, an important regulatory hormone that is normally produced in the human brain. In 1977, researchers at the City of Hope National Medical Center in Los Angeles and at the University of California at San Francisco succeeded in using bacteria to make somatostatin. It is a protein consisting of a sequence of only 14 amino acids. Given this knowledge, they could manufacture a sequence of nucleotides that would code for somatostatin.

The scientists inserted artificial somatostatin-coding DNA into plasmids in billions of *E. coli* bacteria. Thereafter the bacteria made a substance new to them. Actually, what they produced was the protein they had always made connected to somatostatin. This complex protein can then be cut chemically to yield pure human somatostatin.

The point of it all? Somatostatin is a valuable hormone and is needed for the treatment of several disorders in humans. Even though we *(Continued on page 144)*

# GENETIC ENGINEERING: RECOMBINING DNA IN THE LAB

*Explorations in the new biology yield potentially life-saving results in the field of genetic engineering. One method employs billions of E. coli bacteria to produce a desired protein. At Cetus Corporation in Berkeley, California, scientists manufacture interferon, an antiviral protein made naturally, but in minute quantities, by human cells. Laboratory-produced interferon offers hope in the fight against viral diseases. In one experiment, research associate Mike Wu (below at*

*right) prepares to inject frog eggs with "engineered"* E. coli *DNA. If the eggs begin to produce interferon, he will know the bacteria successfully incorporated the complete gene. With a few alterations of the DNA, batches of similarly tested bacteria can produce quantities of interferon. Below at left, biochemical engineer Wolf Hanisch checks the gauge of a cell concentrator containing* E. coli *bacteria. A control panel monitors conditions in the cylindrical tank*

*(background), filled with* E. coli *cells producing human interferon. Later, scientists test the interferon's potency in varying concentrations (below, lower photograph); cells stained purple, protected by bacteria-manufactured interferon, survived a viral attack.*

PAGES 142-143: *Technician Leigh Scalapino examines tissue cultures in a "clean room," a sterile lab that reduces the chances of contamination.*

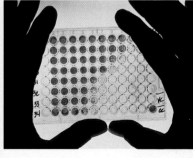

know its chemical composition, it is expensive to synthesize in the laboratory. But once the bacterial culture that makes it has been developed, it can be produced in large quantities at much lower cost.

Genetic engineering is creating an entirely new industry. Pioneering companies have been springing up, and a few of these private firms are now mounting joint efforts with university scientists. Stanford and the University of California at Berkeley recently entered into contracts with a group of genetic-engineering companies in the San Francisco Bay area. Such agreements between private enterprise and the scientific establishment assure greater resources for research and development along with new capabilities for rapidly producing useful new products.

The age of genetic engineering has only begun. The possibilities it suggests for improvements in human life seem almost without limit. As David Baltimore, the Nobel prizewinning geneticist at Massachusetts Institute of Technology, says: "We're close to being able to know just about anything we want to know about molecular genetics. . . . in the foreseeable future, we will understand cancer, genetic disease, aging, and the development and function of the nervous system." By foreseeable future, Baltimore does not mean tomorrow or next year. It is simply that we are now confident that our major questions about the human organism will someday be answered.

But there is much more to the new biology than genetic engineering. One fascinating development in molecular biology is the discovery that a cell, under certain conditions, can generate extra copies of its existing genes. This work is being done by my Stanford colleague Robert Schimke, chairman of the Department of Biological Sciences, and his associates. It was known for some time that methotrexate, or MTX, a drug used in treating cancer, works only for a while; then the cancer becomes resistant to it. MTX kills cancer cells by inactivating an enzyme in the cells, but the cancer cell can counter the drug by producing much more of the enzyme. One way to make more of the enzyme would be for the cells to have more of that part of the DNA that codes for the enzyme.

Schimke's group treated cultured mouse cells with gradually increasing doses of MTX, and developed cell lines that were as much as 500 times as resistant to MTX as the original cells. In one of the resistant cell lines, a much larger chromosome developed in the nucleus—twice the size of any in normal cells. This larger chromosome contained many additional copies of the gene that codes for production of the enzyme. Thus the cells produce much more of the enzyme, and the MTX cannot inactivate all of it. The cells have literally evolved a new piece of chromosome.

How this happens—how genes are regulated and controlled to express their messages and even to increase their number—is one of the most intriguing questions of the new biology.

The process by which a human being develops from a single fertilized cell has been one of the profound mysteries of science. People often suppose that a complete "blueprint" of the person is present in the genetic material of the chromosomes, but that is not so. Stanford's Norman Wessells, an eminent developmental biologist, likes to use an analogy suggested by Donald Kennedy. The DNA writes the "prime contract." It specifies the plan for the building blocks (the proteins) and the basic rules for the way the job should be done. But additional "specifications" are present in the cell outside the nucleus. Specialized materials in various parts of the fertilized cell provide "subcontracts" with essential stipulations. Later, as tissues develop, the interactions among them result in still more specific subcontracts.

To take one example, the fertilized frog-egg cell contains a specialized part called the gray crescent. When the cell starts to divide, normally the first cleavage, or beginning of separation, goes through the gray crescent so that each of the two new cells retains a portion of it, and development is normal. If we separate these two cells entirely, each will develop into a normal tadpole, resulting in identical twins.

If, however, we alter the cleavage so that all the gray crescent ends up in one cell and none in the other, only the cell with the gray crescent will develop into a tadpole. The gray crescent lies outside the nucleus and contains no DNA. Yet it critically affects development. It is true, of course, that DNA was necessary for the development of the gray crescent in the first place. But our example shows that DNA's influence is not completely centralized.

Separation of the single frog egg led to the development of two frogs, containing identical genes. Researchers in embryology set out to apply this principle of nature to the reproduction, by asexual means, of large numbers of organisms that would be genetically identical—a process called cloning.

One procedure, nuclear transplantation, first requires the removal of the nucleus of a cell, usually taken from an embryo. This nucleus is then delicately placed in an egg of the same species whose own nucleus has been removed. This is relatively easy with frogs and fish, because their eggs are comparatively large and develop outside the body. It is much more difficult with mammals, but was finally accomplished in 1979 when nuclear transplants resulted in the birth of three healthy mice in Switzerland.

More recently, using a quite different approach, researchers at the University of Oregon learned to clone zebra fish on a large scale, hatching as many as 200 identical baby fish at a time. The new technique manipulates embryos in such a way that the young fish always contain the same combination of genes.

Theoretically, laboratory cloning of human beings is now technically possible; but it seems highly unlikely, in light of the moral and political constraints that influence social policy. As someone has said, great financial rewards have already come from human cloning experiments—but only to writers of science fiction!

Much of the new biology, of course, is science fiction becoming fact. Both cloning and genetic engineering may one day help us answer the old question: How much is behavior determined by genetic makeup, and how much is it determined by external influences? We are only at the beginning, but the new biology has already contributed substantially to our understanding of life and its complex processes; and it promises much more for our future benefit.

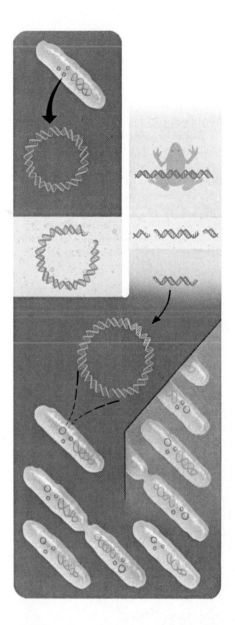

*Adding phrases to DNA's message, scientists can alter genetic makeup. From top: A "restriction enzyme" cuts open a ring of DNA, called a plasmid, from an E. coli bacterium; a segment of frog DNA, bonded to the plasmid's open ends, reforms the ring. After insertion of the plasmid into a new E. coli, the organism divides. This and each succeeding generation of bacteria will reproduce the recombinant, or hybrid, plasmid—retaining the new message.*

# DNA: SPIRAL STAIRCASE TO FUTURE DISCOVERIES

*Knowing the location of a gene within a chromosome may lead to early detection of hereditary disorders. At the Genentech lab in San Francisco, scientist Howard Levine (below) collects purified interferon produced by recombinant DNA for analysis. A process called gel electrophoresis separates DNA fragments—dyed for observation (below, right)—according to molecular size: Shorter ones travel farther through the gel. After radioactive labeling of the sized molecules, Art Franke (lower right) studies photographic film revealing the DNA sequence of a human gene. Opposite, biochemist Herbert Boyer, a pioneer in genetic engineering and a cofounder of Genentech, gazes at a vial of recombinant DNA. The possibilities locked inside seem only as limited as the human imagination.*

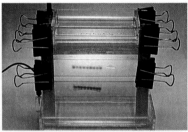

# ADVANCES IN MEDICAL SCIENCE

*By* ANTHONY CERAMI, *Ph.D.*
*Professor of Biochemistry,*
*The Rockefeller University*

We may be growing used to miracles. I have often wondered what my great-grandparents would have thought if someone had told them we would one day be able to transplant a living kidney from one person to another, or replace a damaged heart valve with one made of metal and plastic. And yet these operations are now performed regularly in hospitals around the world.

Today we can prevent or cure diseases that killed thousands only a generation or two ago. In my own lifetime we have developed wondrous new drugs and built sophisticated machines that are aiding in our fight against disease. We have unlocked secrets of genetics that are throwing new light on the causes of illness. We have discovered the critical protective role of the immune system, the body's natural defense mechanism.

Ongoing medical research continues to yield insights into age-old mysteries of the human body. As just one example, at Rockefeller University my colleagues and I are studying a question that has long intrigued humanity: Is there a way to keep the body from aging? Our studies have convinced us that aging can be likened to the process that takes place when food is cooked. As everyone knows, when you roast a chicken it turns brown. The brown pigments are the result of a

*Position fixed precisely by laser beams, a cancer patient awaits a brain scan at Los Alamos National Laboratory in New Mexico. Doctors will bombard his tumor with subatomic particles. Slowly, such experimental treatments extend the frontiers of medical knowledge.*

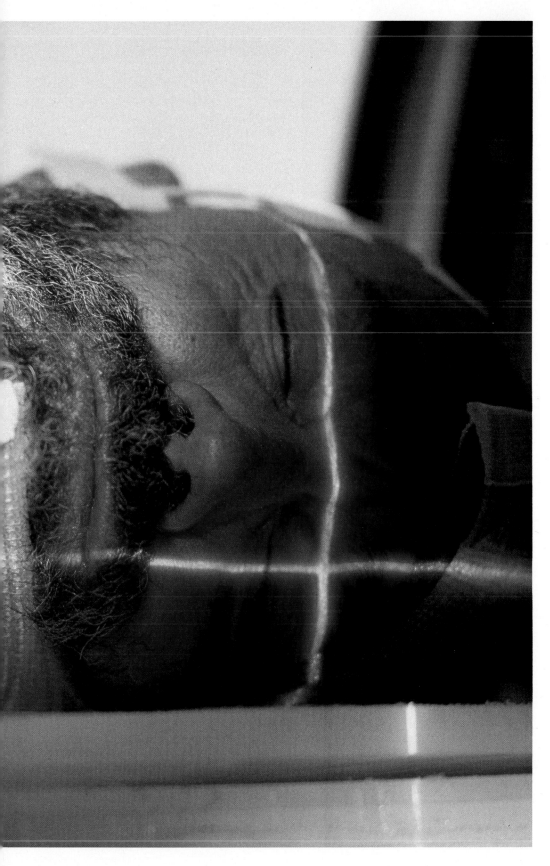

## ASSAULT ON CANCER: HUGE MACHINES, MINUTE PARTICLES

*Nuclear-age machines developed for physics research unleash their force against cancer at Los Alamos. Starting the process, a pillared, multistoried generator (opposite) gives protons—the nuclei of hydrogen atoms—a 750,000-volt jolt. As a technician records procedures (below), the protons hurtle through an injection tube and pass into a half-mile-long linear accelerator, where they attain nearly the speed of light. Crashing into target atoms along the way, the proton barrage frees smaller particles called pi-mesons—pions for short—which doctors then aim at the tumors of cancer patients. Pions, they theorize, cause minute explosions in malignancies, while sparing most of the healthy tissue. During sessions lasting up to 40 minutes, patients wear fiberglass casts to hold them steady. At left, above, low-level ultraviolet light hardens the materials in a patient's newly molded cast; stored between treatments, casts at left resemble headgear for science fiction wars.*

1       2       3       4

*Grim duel, magnified 9,000 times, pits white blood cells against a cancer cell. From left: Killer T cells— part of the body's natural immune system—attach themselves to a single, larger malignant tumor cell (1). Contact triggers the tumor cell's own defense (2): the formation of blisters or vesicles on the cell's surface. With T cell attached, vesicles enlarge (3); leaving the cancer cell, they begin to fasten onto the T cell (4 and 5). As dozens of vesicles cluster about the T cell (6), they form a barrier between it and the tumor cell (7). Finally, the wall of vesicles isolates the T cell and drives it away from the cancer cell (8), which, though damaged, survives. The outcome varies, however. Sometimes cancer cells succumb to such attacks.*

reaction between glucose and protein in the flesh of the chicken. Our research has shown that humans also "brown."

In humans, this browning happens at 37°C (98.6°F) and takes place over a lifetime. Browning is especially pronounced in parts of the body where new proteins are not formed. In many parts of the body, such as the outside of the skin or the blood cells, proteins are constantly being replaced. But in the basic structure that is *you*—your bones and joints, for example—proteins are not replaced after the parts are built.

The proteins in the lens of the eye are formed before we are born, and are never replaced. Some of the vision problems of old age may be linked to the gradual browning of these proteins. I once gave a talk on this subject, and a man from the audience told me that he finally understood why the vibrant paintings of French impressionist Claude Monet had changed so dramatically. Late in his life, Monet had had cataracts removed. Before the operation, his paintings had become darker; afterward they were bright once again. The man speculated that Monet must have been seeing a "brown" world caused by dark pigments in the lenses of his eyes.

I first encountered the browning phenomenon in my studies of diabetes. At Rockefeller we have measured the amount of brown pigment in diabetics and found that, in this regard, such people are often significantly "older" than their actual ages. We have found 35-year-old diabetics who have as much brown pigment as a normal person of 70 or 80 years. The diabetics brown, or age, faster than the normal individual because of their higher blood glucose levels.

Realizing this, we looked for a way

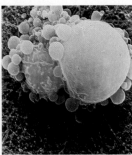

6 7 8

to monitor the browning process in these patients. In 1975 one of my doctoral students, Ron Koenig, and I developed a test to measure the protein glycohemoglobin. Now used worldwide, this test helps gauge the extent of the reactions between glucose and proteins. The test can show whether a patient's blood sugar level has been properly controlled over a period of up to 30 days, thus aiding in the management of diabetes.

We now think that many of the complications of aging may be due to the browning process. Our research has shown that when glucose reacts with a protein, it binds the molecules of the protein together, making them tougher and less flexible—just as in food that's been overcooked. The hardening of the arteries or the stiffening of the tissue of the lungs may come about in this way. Our hope is that in time we shall be able to slow the aging of some parts of the body by interfering with this process.

While research in areas such as aging is still in its early stages, the struggle against many of the diseases that afflict mankind has been going on for hundreds of years. One of man's greatest foes has always been infectious disease. Massive epidemics once raged across the earth unchecked. In the Middle Ages bubonic plague, the dreaded Black Death, repeatedly ravaged Europe, and in the 14th century alone killed an estimated one-third of the population.

The first effective protection against such calamities came in the 18th century with the development of a vaccine for smallpox. Edward Jenner, an English country doctor, noticed that milkmaids seemed immune to the dread disease. He reasoned that the young women

contracted the less virulent cowpox and subsequently developed an immunity to smallpox. By the 1790s experiments had proved his theory correct, and vaccination with cowpox virus soon gained widespread acceptance.

Jenner's work was followed by a number of significant breakthroughs against infectious disease. Perhaps the most important was the discovery of the relationship between bacteria and disease—the so-called "germ theory" elaborated by Louis Pasteur and Robert Koch in the late 1870s. From the 1880s on, researchers identified and studied the causes of numerous infectious diseases, and in many cases they were able to develop effective vaccines.

The second half of the 19th century saw rapid gains in other methods of dealing with health hazards. Improved water and sewage systems helped reduce waterborne infections such as cholera and typhus. And in the first half of this century, methods for controlling disease-bearing mosquitoes sharply reduced the toll of malaria and yellow fever.

In the last three or four decades the impact of medicine and public health practices has become even greater. Chemical agents such as sulfa drugs and antibiotics have been used with increasing effectiveness in combating infectious diseases. With the establishment of bodies such as the World Health Organization, the latest information in disease detection, treatment, and prevention is being made available even in remote areas. The result of these advances has been the elimination or control of many age-old scourges. Smallpox has effectively been wiped from the face of the earth. There has been no outbreak of cholera in the United States since early in

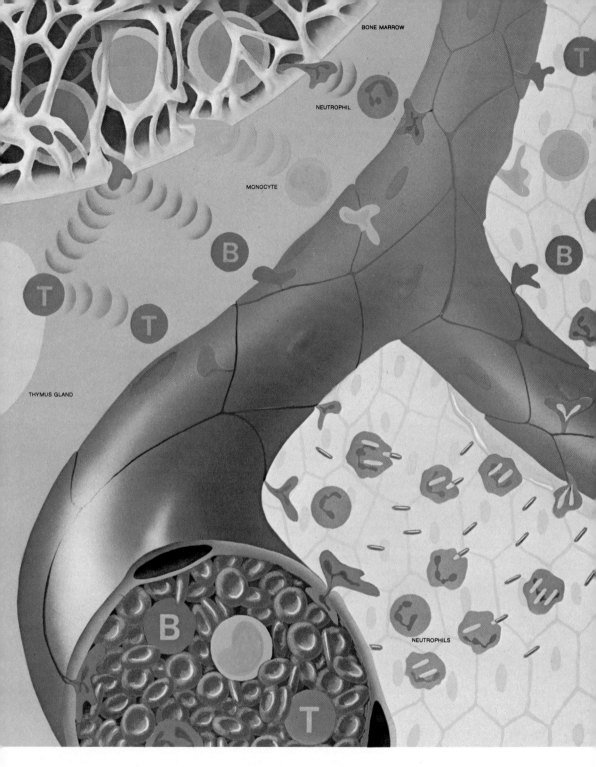

BONE MARROW

NEUTROPHIL

MONOCYTE

THYMUS GLAND

NEUTROPHILS

## THE IMMUNE SYSTEM
## AT WORK

*Microscopic armadas, white blood cells wage war against disease-causing invaders in a simplified representation of the immune response. B lymphocytes, neutrophils, and monocytes originate in the bone marrow; T lymphocytes develop from cells that detour to the thymus. These white cells migrate*

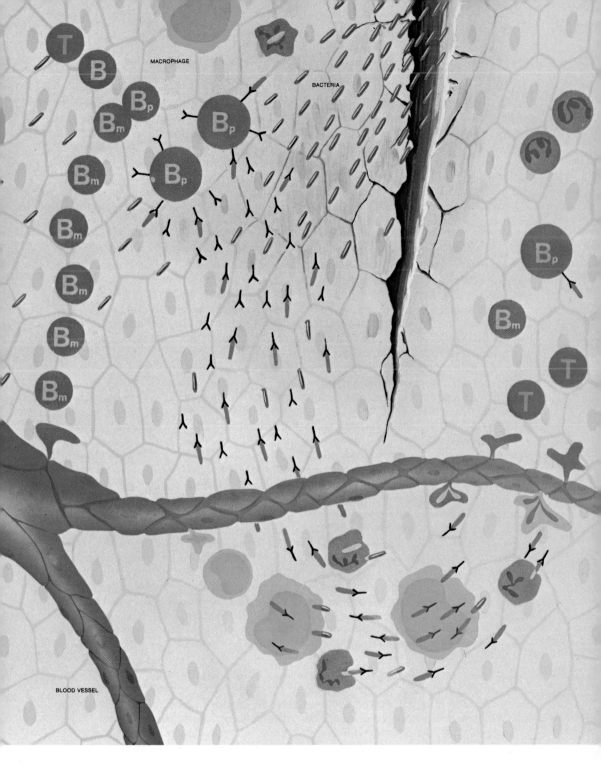

MACROPHAGE

BACTERIA

BLOOD VESSEL

*through the body via blood vessels.
As bacteria enter through a cut (upper
right), neutrophils engage the enemy.
Overwhelmed, they send out a chemical
alert (lower center). Aided by T cells,
B cells divide into two types: plasma (Bp)
cells, which secrete Y-shaped antibody
molecules, and memory (Bm) cells,*

*prepared to defend against similar
future threats. Antibodies lock onto the
bacteria's antigens—"recognition
sites"—and neutralize the intruders.
Macrophages (enlarged monocytes) and
neutrophils consume the debris (lower
right). T cells suppress antibody
production as the skirmish ends.*

155

this century. The development of drugs to treat tuberculosis has resulted in the closing of hundreds of sanatoriums.

The fight against infectious disease goes on, however, for these illnesses are still the world's main cause of death. Tuberculosis alone continues to kill some 3.5 million people a year. New strains of bacteria and viruses have developed, including bacteria resistant to formerly effective "wonder" drugs. Penicillin-resistant organisms, for example, are becoming commonplace, forcing pharmacologists constantly to adjust the chemical composition of penicillin. Some new bacteria actually *require* the presence of once deadly drugs for their growth.

Nevertheless, infectious diseases are no longer the threat they were at the beginning of this century. The reduction of deaths from these maladies has produced a significant increase in life expectancy, particularly in developed nations. Average life expectancy in the United States has risen from 47 to 74 in the last 80 years. (This dramatic increase appears to have leveled off recently.) As people have tended to live longer, other kinds of sicknesses have become dominant in determining the length of life. Over the last few decades the incidence of cardiovascular disease has been increasing. Heart attacks and strokes are now the biggest killers in the United States, claiming more than 700,000 lives a year.

The cardiovascular system, along with the lungs, provides the continuous exchange of oxygen and carbon dioxide that is essential to human life. All our cells require oxygen to function, and the carbon dioxide they produce as a waste product must be eliminated. The arteries carry oxygen-rich blood away from the heart, branching into ever smaller vessels. The smallest arteries deliver blood to the capillaries, which have walls a single cell thick. The exchange of oxygen and carbon dioxide between the blood and the tissues takes place at this level. From the capillaries, blood containing carbon dioxide returns to the heart through the veins.

Each contraction of the heart is sparked by a tiny electrical impulse within the heart muscle. At rest, the heart pumps about 70 times a minute, or some 100,000 times in a day. About five quarts of blood pass through the heart every minute; during exercise this can increase to 35 quarts. Obviously the heart must be remarkably strong to perform this amount of work throughout an individual's lifetime. However, cardiovascular disease can prevent the heart from functioning normally.

One of the most prevalent such diseases is atherosclerosis, the buildup of fatty deposits known as plaque inside an artery. Made up of cholesterol and scar tissue, these deposits can slow the flow of blood and can grow until they cut off oxygen and nutrients, resulting in the death of tissue. If this happens in a vital blood vessel, the results can be devastating. Blockage of an artery to the brain can lead to stroke; blockage of one of the arteries that supply blood to the heart muscle itself can result in heart attack.

Several factors appear to be directly related to cardiovascular problems. The most important are cigarette smoking and hypertension, both associated with heart attacks. The amounts of cholesterol and other saturated fats consumed relate to atherosclerosis. Diabetes also increases the risk of cardiovascular disease, as may stress and lack of exercise.

In the last decade, greater attention to controlling these factors, along with improved methods of diagnosis and treatment, has helped cut the death rate from heart attack in the United States by 25 percent, and from stroke by nearly 40 percent. New diagnostic tools, such as thermography and nuclear scanning, are giving doctors a nonsurgical look inside the human body, enabling them to detect tissues with endangered circulation and to see the heart at work.

Many drugs aimed at helping diseased hearts have been introduced in the last several years, as well as new medicines to control contributing ailments such as diabetes and hypertension. We have developed drugs to deal with blood clots. In experimental use with heart attack victims, one of these—streptokinase—has dissolved arterial clots in less than an hour. A group of drugs called beta blockers was introduced in the United States in the 1970s. These drugs prevent nerve impulses from reaching sites called beta receptors in the heart and the

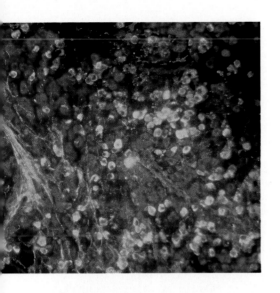

*Under ultraviolet light, fluorescent dyes illuminate antibody-producing plasma cells in the spleen of a mouse. Those glowing red make one type of antibody, important in the early immune response; the green produce another antibody that survives longer in the bloodstream. The cells' specialized reactions hint at the entire immune system's incredibly varied and specific responses: In the same way that one key unlocks only one door, one kind of antibody reacts against just one of an almost infinite number of antigens. Scientists now believe the human body capable of producing millions of distinct antibodies.*

blood vessels. They are now used to prevent recurring heart attacks, to reduce blood pressure, and to control arrhythmia—irregular heartbeat—and angina, a condition caused by insufficient blood flow through coronary arteries.

Another group of new drugs, the calcium blockers, helps control the rate and the force of heartbeats by slowing the flow of calcium ions into the cells of the heart muscle. Calcium blockers are being used to treat hypertension, arrhythmia, and angina, as well as coronary artery spasms, contractions that temporarily cut off the flow of blood. These spasms, which can occur even in healthy arteries, are especially dangerous in patients suffering from atherosclerosis.

Surgical techniques for the treatment of heart defects have also improved greatly in recent years. Many heart patients suffer from arrhythmia. The introduction of artificial pacemakers in the 1950s gave us a way of correcting this condition. Electrodes implanted in the heart muscle and connected to a power source provide a steady series of electrical impulses, restoring the heart's normal rhythm. About a million Americans have been fitted with pacemakers.

A landmark in heart surgery came in 1967, when specialists at the Cleveland Clinic in Ohio performed the first coronary bypass operation. The surgeons were able to relieve a blocked coronary artery by using a vein taken from the patient's leg to detour blood around the obstructed portion of the artery. Some 100,000 bypass operations are now performed yearly in the United States.

A new surgical technique that holds considerable promise for treating blocked coronary arteries is balloon angioplasty. In this procedure, doctors insert a catheter into an artery in the patient's arm or leg. They guide the catheter through the artery to the blocked area. They then feed a small tube with a tiny balloon on the end through the catheter. By inflating the balloon inside the blocked passage, the surgeons attempt to open the artery. This technique has proven effective in a significant percentage of operations, and may offer a quicker and cheaper alternative to bypass surgery for many patients. Other techniques for treating—and *(Continued on page 162)*

# CELL SORTERS
# SPEED
# RESEARCH

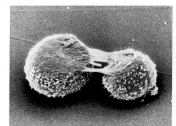

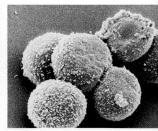

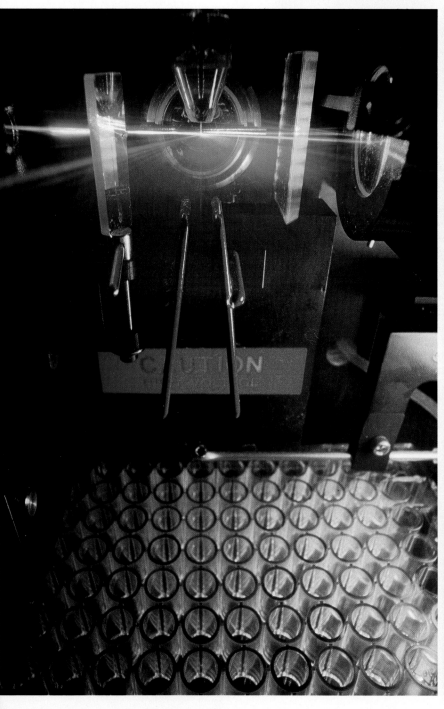

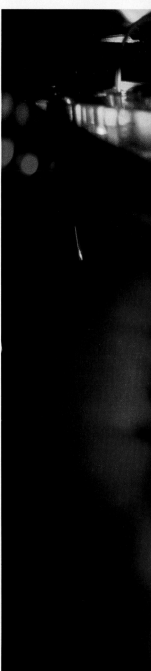

Lightning-fast sorting machines analyze thousands of liquid-borne cells a second. At Lawrence Livermore National Laboratory in California (below), high-voltage plates deflect charged droplets from a stream onto a dish. In a similar apparatus in a Stanford University genetics laboratory, a laser beam detects fluorescence-dyed cells (below, left). Plates divert them into tray wells. Cell sorters can pluck out hybridomas (left), the results of fusing short-lived antibody-producing cells with wildly replicating cancer cells. Nearly immortal, hybridomas make vast amounts of antibodies for research use.

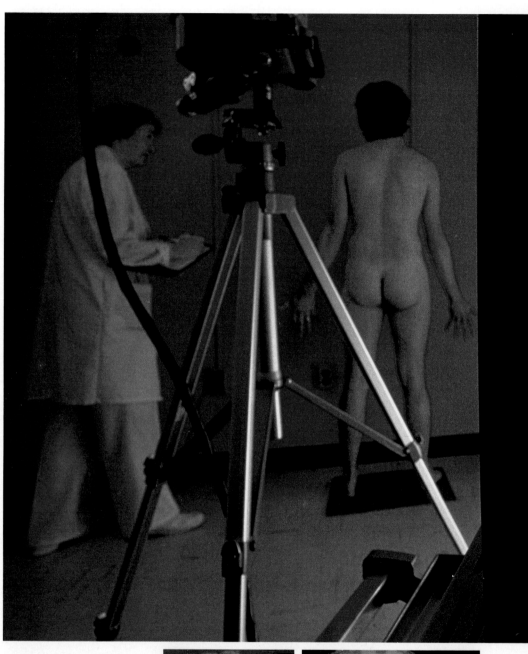

**INFRARED
ALERT**

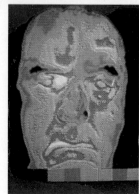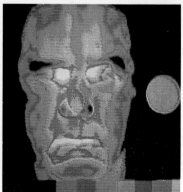

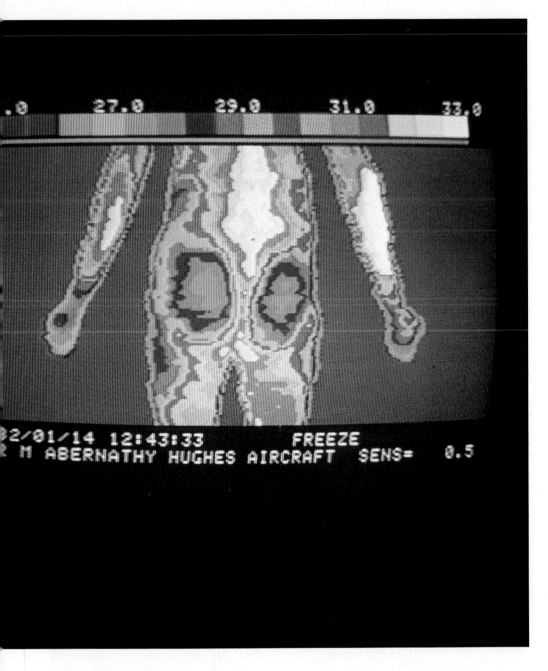

27.0 29.0 31.0 33.0

2/01/14 12:43:33 FREEZE
M ABERNATHY HUGHES AIRCRAFT SENS= 0.5

Body heat and coolness translate into color-coded thermograms, images that aid in the diagnosis of illness and injury ranging from tumor to whiplash. At Georgetown University Medical Center's thermography division in Washington, D. C., nurse Cathryn Robinson helps as a volunteer bares himself to an infrared detector (above, at left). The detector conveys data via computer to the video screen above. At the top of the screen, colors assigned to subtle temperature differences range from coolest, at left, to warmest. Physicians look for asymmetry in thermograms; this subject shows only a sunburn on his right arm. At far left, a cool spot above a patient's left eye reveals impaired circulation—warning of a possible stroke. To avert that threat, surgeons unclogged a narrowed artery in his neck that same night. The post-operative thermogram (near left) shows circulation and symmetry restored.

preventing—cardiovascular disease continue to be perfected. In the years ahead we should experience an even further drop in the cardiovascular mortality rate.

Perhaps even more feared than heart disease, cancer is second to cardiovascular illness in the number of its victims, killing some 430,000 Americans a year. Yet progress is also being made in the detection and treatment of this disease.

Thirty years ago a diagnosis of cancer was often considered a death sentence. Through advances in surgical techniques and improved methods of radiation therapy and chemotherapy, several kinds of cancer can now be completely cured and the growth of others slowed. The death rate from Hodgkin's disease, a malignancy of the lymph nodes, has dropped significantly in the last ten years. From 80 to 90 percent of its victims can now be cured. Childhood leukemia, too, can be defeated in many cases. Testicular and ovarian cancer are often curable today. And, because of the extremely high cure rate, most forms of skin cancer are now omitted from cancer mortality statistics.

Despite these successes, there has been a rise in the cancer mortality rate recently, largely because of the increasing incidence of cancers of the lung and digestive tract. Actually, cancer is not a single disease. The body contains more than a hundred kinds of cells, and each can develop a specific type of cancer. Although cancer can assume many guises, there is a common characteristic in all its forms: an uncontrolled growth of cells. Something happens to a normal cell causing it to multiply, invading surrounding cells. The most dangerous cancer cells are those that spread, or metastasize, forming new colonies in sometimes distant parts of the body.

What causes these cancerous cells to develop in the first place? We now know that many cancers are triggered by environmental factors—substances in the air or in our food or water. The World Health Organization estimates that perhaps 90 percent of all human cancers are caused by environmental agents. The connection between cancer and environment was made as far back as 200 years ago, when English physician Sir Percival Pott noticed the high frequency of skin

*Conception outside the womb brings hope to the childless in Eastern Virginia Medical School's fertility program. Below, a pipette holds an egg cell from a woman's ovary; joined with the husband's sperm, it has divided into three cells (center). Implanted, such embryos develop in the uterus. In 1981, Elizabeth Carr (bottom) became the first American-born baby conceived by this method, known as* in vitro *fertilization.*

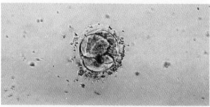

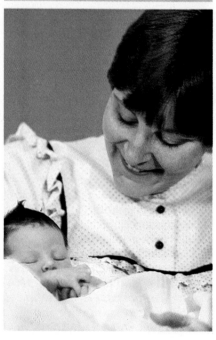

cancer in chimney sweeps. The sweeps, usually young boys, were exposed to chimney soot containing the carcinogenic chemical benzopyrene.

Since then we have made many other connections between cancer and environmental factors. One of the most important was the discovery of the link between lung cancer and smoking; smoking is now believed to cause more than a fourth of all cancer deaths. It is now apparent that some people are particularly susceptible to cancer-causing chemicals. Development of routine screening techniques for this vulnerability could some day alert such people to avoid exposure to potential carcinogens.

Certain kinds of radiation also can cause cancer. The most common form, of course, is sunlight, which causes by far the greatest number of tumors in humans. Fortunately, most of these skin tumors are easily treated. Viruses, too, have been shown to cause cancer in laboratory animals, although it has not been proved that they cause human cancers.

**R**ecent research has been aimed at determining how carcinogenic agents cause a normal cell to change into a cancer cell. Although this change could be nothing more than a random event, many researchers feel that carcinogens cause genetic mutations—alterations in a cell's genetic material, or DNA. A gene or group of genes may result that no longer behaves normally. Once this change takes place, the mutant gene is passed on to each new cell. There may be little difference between the cancer cell and normal cells, but that difference can be fatal.

One provocative insight into the mechanisms of cancer was reported in 1975 by Dr. Beatrice Mintz of the Fox Chase Institute for Cancer Research, in Philadelphia. Dr. Mintz inserted highly malignant cancer cells into mouse embryos, then placed the embryos in the uteruses of foster mothers. Amazingly, the mice that were born were cancer-free. Somehow the normal embryo cells influenced the cancer cells to behave normally. When we learn how this change took place, we will perhaps have a new way of dealing with cancer.

Many scientists believe that everyone produces cancer cells regularly, perhaps every day. But in most instances the body's immune system recognizes these abnormal cells and destroys them before they can form life-threatening tumors. Evidence supports this theory. For example, patients who have received organ transplants must be treated with drugs that suppress their immune systems. Otherwise, their bodies would recognize the transplanted organs as foreign substances and reject them. Records show that these patients face an increased risk of later developing cancer.

The immune system forms a sort of surveillance and combat patrol, ready to fight foreign substances in the body's defense. Pasteur and other 19th-century scientists came to realize that some such system existed. By 1900 researchers had discovered that the human body produces proteins called antibodies to attack foreign substances. But not until the last two decades have we begun to realize the full complexity of the immune system. The chief elements of that system are white blood cells called lymphocytes. Components of the lymph nodes and spleen, lymphocytes are also present in the thymus, blood, bone marrow, and linings of the respiratory and gastrointestinal tracts. B lymphocytes produce specific antibodies; T lymphocytes regulate B cell activity.

Other white blood cells, called macrophages, ingest foreign material and help stimulate B cells. Macrophages also have an additional role, one only recently discovered. For years I wondered why chronic diseases such as cancer can cause a tremendous weight loss. Many times the loss is out of proportion to the size of the tumor. We began studying this problem a few years ago at Rockefeller University and have found that whenever the body is invaded, a special protein is made by the macrophages and released into the blood. This protein turns off the body's energy storage functions, making more energy available to the immune system to fight the invasion.

In a simple incursion, such as a minor cut in which a few bacteria enter the body, this energy mobilization may last only a few days. Afterward the body resumes its normal functions of building muscle tissue and storing fat. With a chronic problem *(Continued on page 168)*

# THE VERSATILE
# MEDICAL LASER

*Accurately guided rays of the laser find
widening medical uses: They can weld,
drill, or vaporize diseased tissues, and
their use often replaces conventional
surgery, especially in eye ailments.
At New York's Beth Israel Medical Center,
Dr. Maurice Luntz (below, at right) aims
an argon-gas laser into the eye of a*

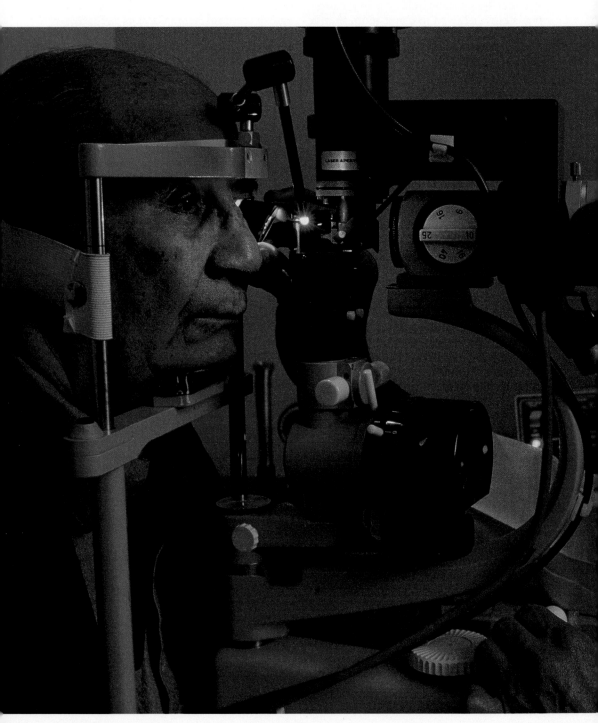

glaucoma patient. *Instantly and almost painlessly, the laser burns tiny spots in his eye to help drain blocked fluid and relieve pressure. Argon lasers mainly affect red-pigmented areas; other types of lasers affect tissues of different colors. At right, top, a mosaic of perhaps 2,000 laser burns speckles a retina and halts* abnormal blood vessel growth caused by diabetes (camera lights glow yellow at the left). In the center photograph, hemorrhaging behind a retina distorts normal eyesight. Two months after krypton laser treatments, with vision preserved, only healthy scar tissue remains to mark the spot (bottom).*

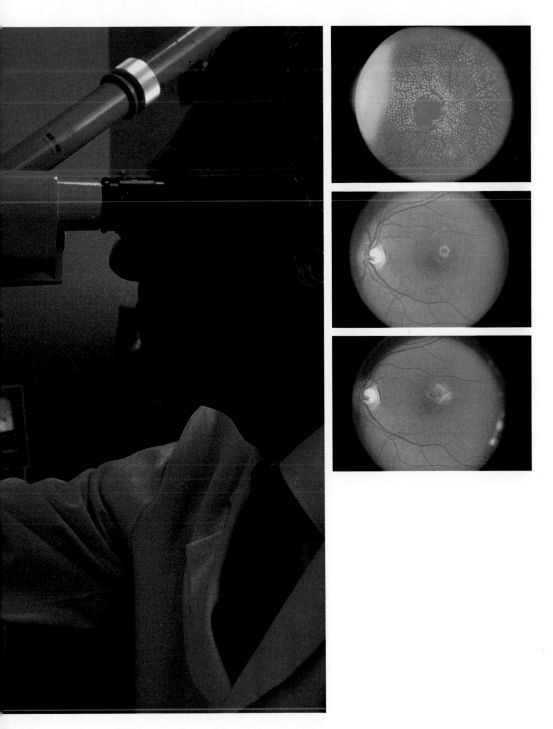

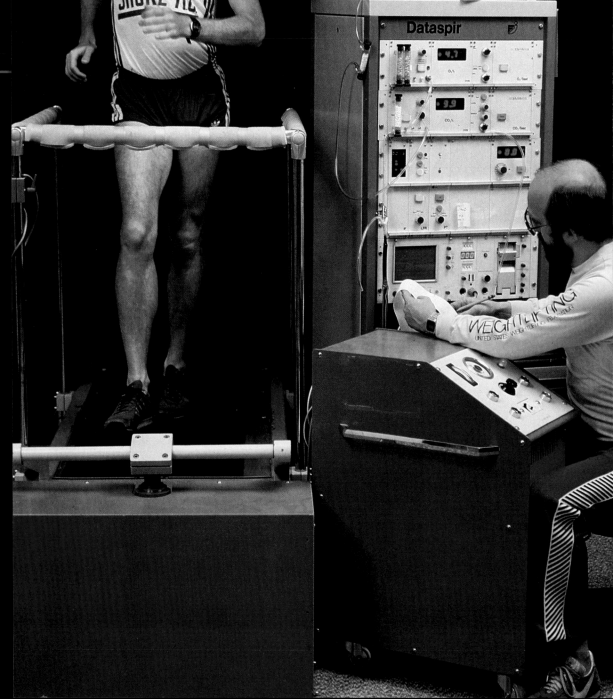

# THE GROWING FIELD OF SPORTS MEDICINE

Sport meets science at the U. S. Olympic Training Center in Colorado Springs, Colorado, where an array of equipment monitors the performance of athletes. On the treadmill at left, walker Leonard Jansen undergoes testing of the work capacity of his lungs. His breathing apparatus directs exhaled air into a computerized unit measuring concentrations of oxygen and carbon dioxide. Dr. Peter Van Handel reads the printout. As Mary Mitchell draws a bowstring (right), sensors analyze wrist movements, which appear on a screen; such information pinpoints inefficient motion and positions, helping improve technique. Grimacing with exertion, judo competitor Pam Cave (below) pushes her leg against a strength-testing lever attached to data-encoders.

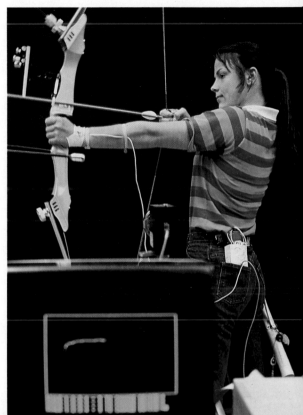

such as a tumor, however, the immune system cannot destroy the invader. Consequently the macrophages keep signaling for more energy. Reserves of muscle and fat are depleted and, in effect, the body consumes itself.

In our laboratory, we have succeeded in isolating the protein that triggers this energy drain. We hope to find a way of switching off this protein in patients with chronic illnesses so their condition is not made worse by a continuing weight loss. We also hope to develop a test to detect the protein in patients with unspecified complaints. If the protein is found in a patient's blood, the physician will know the macrophages are signaling that some sort of invasion is under way.

Much of the current cancer research is aimed at discovering more about how the various parts of the immune system work. Perhaps someday we will be able to stimulate the body's natural defense mechanism to destroy all cancer cells that arise in the body; or we may even develop an anticancer vaccine.

**M**ore and more scientists believe clues to curing cancer and other diseases are to be found in our genes. The hereditary nature of certain illnesses has been in evidence for centuries. But not until the 1950s did we begin to decipher the intricate workings of heredity. In the last three decades new knowledge has advanced our understanding of the structure and function of genetic material at the molecular level. These gains are helping us understand many genetic diseases.

More than 3,000 genetic disorders afflict man. On the average, most humans have at least five or six potentially harmful hereditary traits encoded in their genes in a recessive or "carrier" state. Cystic fibrosis, for example, is transmitted from parent to offspring by recessive genes. Only if both husband and wife bear the same recessive gene can their children suffer the disease. The chance of this occurring is relatively low. In some areas of the world, however, certain mutant genes are common, and there is a high risk of having an afflicted child. In southern Italy and Greece, for example, there is a high incidence of the genetic blood disease called beta-thalassemia, a severe anemic condition.

Our growing knowledge of genetics has created a new medical service: genetic screening and counseling. Scientists can now identify carriers of harmful genes and assess their chances of having an abnormal child. Genetic screening is making it possible for many couples with family histories of genetic disorders to have children without fear. Counseling is an important complement to screening, for it gives prospective parents a clear understanding of genetic disease. They may then avoid psychological problems should they actually have an afflicted child. Counseling can help remove the guilt or shame such parents often feel.

Genetic screening also enables physicians to detect some fetal abnormalities during pregnancy. Tests can reveal the condition of fetuses carried by women known to be at risk for specific diseases—such as women in their late 30s, who are more likely to have a child with Down's syndrome, a mental retardation caused by an abnormal number of chromosomes. Down's syndrome can be detected by examining fetal cells in a sample of amniotic fluid, the liquid surrounding the fetus.

To obtain the sample the physician inserts a needle through the abdominal wall into the uterus and draws off some fluid, a procedure known as amniocentesis. Besides Down's syndrome, amniocentesis can detect Tay-Sachs disease, a fatal degenerative disorder of the nervous system; galactosemia, the inability to metabolize milk sugar; and dozens of other genetic disorders. We can determine fetal status by other tests as well, including ultrasound imaging and blood examinations. The list of genetic diseases revealed by such tests continues to grow.

When tests reveal that a fetus suffers a severe genetic disorder, the parents, forewarned, can prepare for a possibly difficult delivery and for the ongoing problems of a handicapped child. Some people may terminate the pregnancy early through elective abortion. Though effective treatments exist for some genetic diseases, there are currently no cures. But many scientists are optimistic that continuing advances in molecular biology and fetal surgery will eventually give us a way to combat genetic defects.

Another subject relating to human

reproduction, the problem of infertility, has seen an exciting development in recent years, one that holds great promise for couples unable to have children. This development was heralded on July 25, 1978, by the birth of Louise Brown—the world's first "test tube" baby. Her arrival in good health proved that an egg fertilized outside the human body and placed in the womb can lead to a successful pregnancy resulting in a normal baby.

British doctors Robert Edwards and Patrick Steptoe performed the fertilization procedure by removing an egg from one of the ovaries of Mrs. Lesley Brown and placing it in a laboratory dish. There the physicians fertilized the egg with the sperm of Mrs. Brown's husband, John. The embryo that resulted was quickly placed inside Mrs. Brown's uterus, where normal gestation occurred.

This technique, known as *in vitro* (literally, "in glass") fertilization, was developed for use in women whose fallopian tubes are obstructed or have been removed, and therefore cannot transport eggs from the ovaries to the uterus. Several variations of *in vitro* fertilization are now in use, and an increasing number of successful pregnancies have resulted.

As I think about the many advances in medical research made during the last few years, I can't help wondering what lies ahead. The thrilling achievements of recent decades are certain to be matched by additional gains in knowledge. I envision a future in which the riddles of those diseases that still plague us are at last deciphered. I see a day when we will be able to determine to what illnesses a person is genetically susceptible, when we will know how to "talk" to diseased cells and reprogram them, when we will be able to slow the aging of vital organs.

I am hopeful that even as these new miracles unfold, we will determine to protect our own well-being through more prudent living habits. We already know that we can reduce the chance of cardiovascular disease by lowering cholesterol intake. Similarly, we know we can greatly lessen the risk of lung cancer simply by not smoking. As we learn about and apply more ways of reducing the risk of illness, the day may come when curing diseases takes a permanent backseat to preventing them.

*Synthetic skin for burn victims gleams in the hands of researcher Mark Sylvester at the Massachusetts Institute of Technology. Glass jars hold foil-wrapped, freeze-dried mixtures of collagen from cowhide and a powder derived from shark cartilage. A protective layer of plastic membrane, bonded to the cartilage-collagen blend, completes each pliable sheet. Eventually the burn patient's own skin cells, nerve fibers, and blood vessels grow again and replace the synthetic material. Experimentally successful, artificial skin poses an alternative to skin grafts from pigs or cadavers, which the patient's body soon rejects. Some 200,000 Americans suffer severe burns each year.*

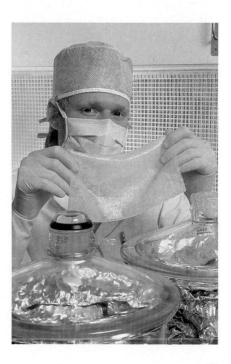

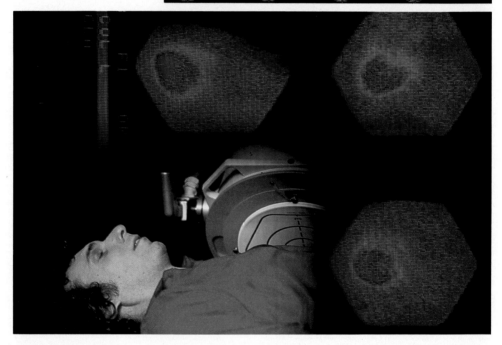

Images of circulating blood in a beating heart, made by nuclear scanning, yield more definitive information than X rays. For such scans, patients receive by vein a radioactive substance that travels to the heart; computer-aided gamma-ray cameras then measure the organ's functioning by recording radioactivity levels in various colors. The progressive scans at top show the left side of the pumping heart as it contracts, then relaxes. Three ten-minute exposures (above) provide views of the muscle of a healthy heart from different angles. In the future, hope for the desperately ill may focus on an artificial heart (opposite). Designed by Dr. Robert Jarvik, left, this 8.8-ounce, plastic-and-aluminum version awaits its first human recipient. Jarvik's colleague at the University of Utah, surgeon William DeVries, right, has implanted a Jarvik model in a calf which then survived for almost nine months.

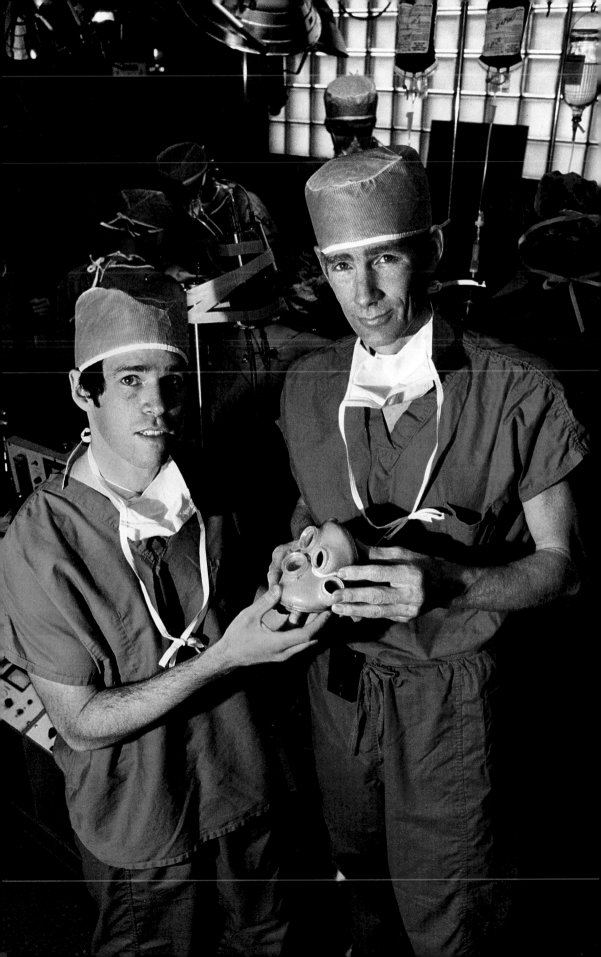

# WONDERS OF THE BRAIN

By SOLOMON H. SNYDER, *M.D.*
*Distinguished Service Professor of*
*Neuroscience, Pharmacology, and Psychiatry,*
*The Johns Hopkins University*

Of all the challenges of science, perhaps the most tantalizing yet most forbidding has been the human brain. Occasionally I remind myself of the drama underlying even the simplest questions about the nervous system—the brain, the spinal cord, and the network of nerves they command. At such moments I may watch myself pick up a book, open it, and begin to read. And I reflect on the thousands of millions of events associated with such a casual action.

First, a thought must have taken form within my brain prompting a desire to read the book. Next came the order to reach over, grasp and lift it, and open the pages. The subtlety of one simple activity of the human hand exceeds the complexities of the most sophisticated computer; so does the visual perception involved in recognizing a few letters on a printed page. Yet picking up the book and seeing some words are minor accomplishments compared with the far more remarkable feat of thinking about the book and formulating the plan to read it.

*Computer-drawn view of a human brain shows twin hemispheres of the cerebrum in red, brain stem in yellow, behind it the cerebellum in orange. Overlapping areas appear white. The computer assembles information from hundreds of brain-tissue photographs in a three-dimensional image.*

PAGES 174-175: *Coached by neuroscientist Robert B. Livingston of the University of California at San Diego, Steve Dixon traces anatomical boundaries for the computer with an electronic cross hair.*

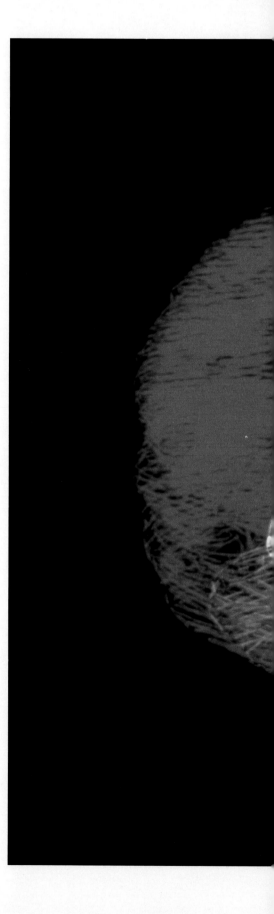

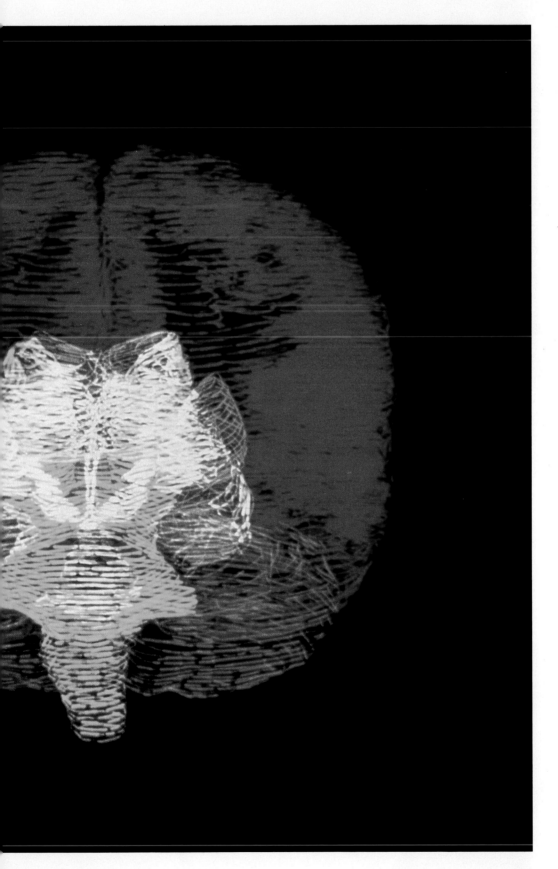

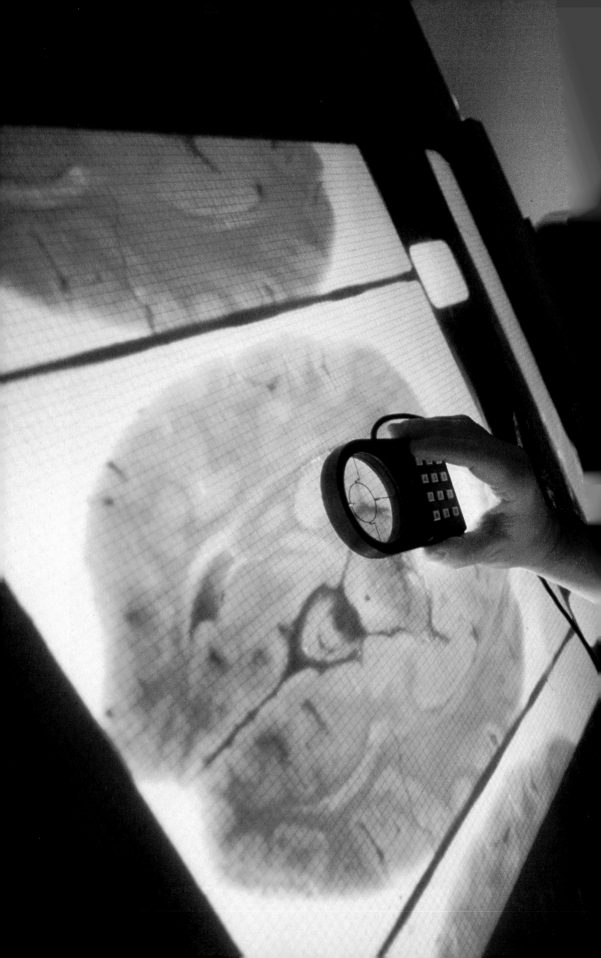

Many scientists are drawn to studies of the brain by just such everyday wonders. There are many other motivations, of course. For me, the attraction began after my first year in medical school, when I stumbled onto a summer job administering psychological tests to psychiatric patients. I did the work at St. Elizabeths Hospital in Washington, D. C., which then housed some 10,000 patients. Their plight frightened me and yet was strangely fascinating. How could human beings made of the same flesh and blood as I was think and behave so differently? What horrifying event or biological damage could cause hallucinations?

My intense interest in schizophrenia, the most severe of mental illnesses, was sparked then and has continued ever since. Along the way, I learned about the development of new drugs that can alter brain functions and alleviate the symptoms of psychotic illness. These seemed to offer the first concrete hope for severely affected mental patients, and prompted my curiosity about how such substances act within the brain—a problem that occupies me still every day.

**K**nowing the structure of the brain is the first step in trying to decipher its functions. Its largest part, the cerebrum, is divided into two hemispheres by a deep fissure. A convoluted mantle called the cerebral cortex covers each hemisphere and seems to dominate the entire structure. The cerebellum, its twin lobes tucked underneath the cerebrum, appears almost as a separate entity. The brain stem is a cylinder projecting from the spinal cord into the cerebrum.

When we compare the brains of different species, we realize that the cerebrum changes remarkably as we move toward the more highly developed animals. Human beings seem to have made a quantum jump in cerebral-cortex size. This great increase suggests that this part of the brain is responsible for the complex and precise perceptions characteristic of humans. Even more important, we can surmise that the cerebral cortex is the organ of that unique human attribute, the ability to reason.

Although most of the brain is involved in receiving sensory information, in storing memories, and in sending out instructions to the muscles, there is nevertheless a fascinating division of labor. The two hemispheres provide several examples. The brain's crossover of signals is such that the left hemisphere controls the activities of the right side of the body, and the right hemisphere the left side of the body. But the hemispheres have divided their functions even more specifically. With most people the left hemisphere is the side of practical thought, dealing with logic, language, and analytical and mathematical processes. The right hemisphere is the stronghold of creative thought—imagination, artistic abilities, perceptions of shapes and colors.

The brain stem regulates such basic aspects of the body's operation as heart rate, blood pressure, and breathing.

As the brain stem ascends, it swells and merges into the hypothalamus. A unique aspect of the hypothalamus is its connection to the pituitary gland, which releases into the bloodstream hormones that regulate activities of the other glands. Only in recent decades was it recognized that the pituitary gland is itself regulated by chemicals manufactured within the hypothalamus. The identification of those substances was a giant step in biomedical research. It linked the electrical activity of nerve cells in the brain with the biochemistry that regulates most bodily functions and behavior.

A British anatomist, the late Geoffrey Harris, was the first to challenge the long-held concept that the pituitary is the ultimate master gland of the body. He felt confident that the brain itself must exert a direct control; but the only link between the two seemed to be the system of small blood vessels connecting the hypothalamus and the pituitary.

By making small knife cuts that selectively damaged those blood vessels, Harris demonstrated obvious interference with pituitary hormone release into the bloodstream. Clearly some chemical must come from the hypothalamus to act upon the pituitary gland.

Scientists reasoned that the hypothalamus must possess "releasing factors" for all of the pituitary's master hormones. But how to find them? Even in animals as large as pigs or sheep, the hypothalamus is so small that one could calculate the amount of a particular releasing factor would be no more than a millionth of a gram! Nevertheless, dozens of research groups attacked the problem. Andrew Schally in New Orleans and Roger Guillemin in Houston led large teams of scientists into the competition. Livestock slaughterhouses all over the southwestern United States supplied hypothalami for extraction.

There followed 15 years of intensive effort, during which each team used up hundreds of thousands of individual hypothalami. In 1969—within weeks of each other—the groups announced the identification and composition of the first releasing factor. Over the next three years, three more were defined. By way of the pituitary, the four factors influence the thyroid, the gonads, and the body's growth mechanisms.

It was a colossal breakthrough. For their achievements, Guillemin and Schally were selected as two of the three recipients of the 1977 Nobel Prize in Physiology or Medicine.

Meanwhile the search proceeds. In 1981 the releasing factor for adrenal cortisol was isolated by a team at the Salk Institute in California led by Dr. Wylie Vale, a former student of Guillemin.

The human brain consists of perhaps 10 to 20 *billion* individual nerve cells, called neurons. The network they form is all the more impressive and intricate because of the nature of each cell. The typical neuron has a long extension called an axon, through which it can send nerve impulses. In addition the cell body puts out hundreds of delicate branches called dendrites; through these it can receive input from more than a thousand other neurons. At the nerve ending, the axon subdivides into as many as 10,000 terminals, each of which can influence a separate neuron. Thus a single one of the brain's billions of nerve cells could conceivably set up several million conversations.

My father has spent his professional career working with computers. We often discuss the challenge of building a machine that could carry out typical brain functions. After considering the number of interactions among neurons in the human brain, we concluded that even with the newest miniaturized microprocessors, a computer that would boast as many connections as the brain

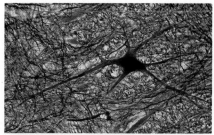

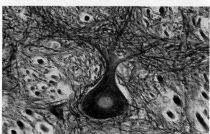

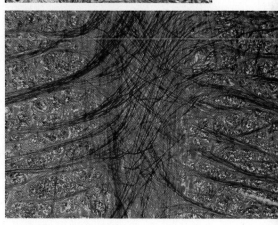

*As varied as human faces and fingertips, the brain's nerve cells, or neurons (top and center), never look exactly alike. But all have in common a cell body and extended fibers: an axon, which transmits impulses to other neurons, and numerous dendrites, which receive messages. The electrochemical signals traversing these circuits form the physical basis of our thought processes and control all bodily activity. Nerve fibers from the two sides of the brain cross each other in the brain stem (bottom photograph), giving each hemisphere control of activities on the opposite side of the body.*

# HOW YOUR COMMAND AND CONTROL CENTER WORKS

*Billions of interconnecting neurons form an immensely complex communications web. This stylized, close-up view represents a minute section of brain tissue. Flow of information in the brain depends on two processes: electrical within the nerve cell, chemical between cells. The lower*

right portion of the painting portrays a chemical transmission. In the bulb-shaped axon ending—one of the axon's thousands of terminals—tiny sacs or vesicles (shown as orange circles) store neurotransmitters (orange dots). When an electrical impulse within a cell reaches an axon ending, vesicles spill their contents into the synapse, a narrow gap between the axon ending and another neuron. The neurotransmitters lock onto specialized receptor sites in the membrane of the receiving cell, initiating a new electrical signal within that neuron.

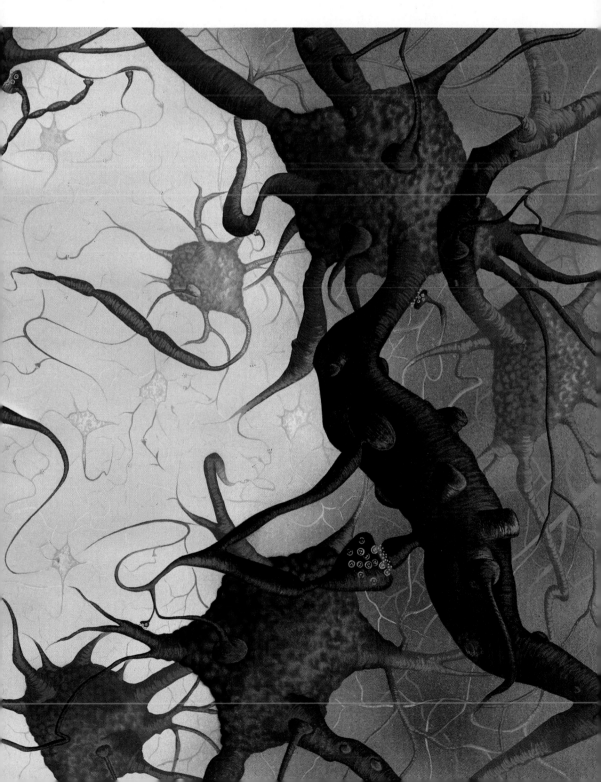

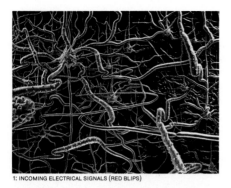

1: INCOMING ELECTRICAL SIGNALS (RED BLIPS)

*Acrylic plastic model of a typical neuron network: (1) Incoming signals speed through dendrites toward the cell body. (2) Impulses raise the cell's electrical potential, indicated by a red glow. (3) When sufficiently charged, the cell body fires (yellow glow), thrusting the impulse along the axon. (4) The message reaches one of the axon's bulbous endings, where it will cross the gap to another nerve cell by means of a chemical transmitter.*

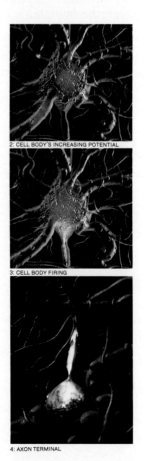

2: CELL BODY'S INCREASING POTENTIAL

3: CELL BODY FIRING

4: AXON TERMINAL

would fill a ten-story building covering an area the size of Texas—approximately 267,000 square miles!

How do the neurons carry out all this communication? A signal from the cell body travels down the axon as an electrical impulse. At the nerve ending, the signal triggers the release of a chemical called a neurotransmitter. The chemical then diffuses across the short gap to an adjacent neuron, and—depending on the kind of transmitter—either stimulates or inhibits electrical activity in that cell.

It was for his demonstration of the chemical link in the body's system of inner communication that Otto Loewi shared a Nobel prize in 1936. He knew that when one stimulates the vagus nerve leading to the heart, that organ beats more slowly. Loewi suspected that a chemical, not simply an electrical connection, controlled this reaction.

He conceived of the ideal experiment to test his theory in a dream one summer night, but the next morning he couldn't remember what it was. That night he put a paper and pencil beside his bed, dreamed again, and upon waking quickly scribbled down some notes. Then he rushed into the laboratory.

Loewi's classic experiment was to bathe a frog's heart in a fluid while the vagus nerve was stimulated. He then immersed the heart of another frog in the fluid—and the beating of the second heart slowed down. Obviously some substance with heart-slowing capability had been released from the nerve. Subsequently Loewi showed that the chemical released into the bath was acetylcholine.

For years scientists assumed that the nervous system needs only two chemical transmitters, one to speed and the other to inhibit the neuron's signal. One of the great advances in brain research in the last decade has been the appreciation that there exist a very large number of neurotransmitters. Presently we know of about 30, and I would estimate that there may in fact be between 100 and 200 of them.

Why is it so important that we learn about each and every one? Of all aspects of brain functioning, it is this one that we can most easily modify medically. The passage of the electrical impulse from the cell body down the axon is an all-or-none process; drugs that influence it are often lethal. By contrast, we can subtly affect the composition or activity of a chemical transmitter. Indeed, every drug we know to affect behavior does so by way of one or another neurotransmitter system.

Studies in this field led logically to the theory that certain chemical transmitters exert their effects in very specific areas of the brain. At Johns Hopkins University, this theory became an important assumption in the search for an opiate-like transmitter.

For thousands of years it has been known that the opium poppy contains substances that can profoundly influence mental functioning. After the discovery and analysis in the 19th century of opium's major active ingredients, morphine and codeine, chemists proceeded to synthesize many opiate drugs that are widely used in clinical medicines.

Besides their role in combating pain, opiates influence emotional behavior, usually creating a sense of well-being. In the 19th century opium extracts were used not only as painkillers but also to relieve anxiety or depression and to promote sleep. The gradual realization that they are addictive caused a restriction of their use to the treatment of severe pain. But if one could develop a nonaddicting opiate, the range of disorders in which these drugs could be employed might be greatly increased.

The striking selectivity and potencies of many opiate drugs indicated to me that they must act at highly specific receptor sites, presumably on the surface of neurons. In 1973 Candace Pert (then a graduate student) and I succeeded in measuring the binding of certain opiates—made radioactive for the purpose—to brain membranes. Our findings were confirmed independently by other investigators.

Subsequent research greatly clarified how opiates act. For instance, Dr. Pert and Michael Kuhar at Johns Hopkins developed a technique whereby we can observe interactions of drugs and receptors at a microscopic level.

It turned out that opiate receptors are not distributed diffusely all over the brain. Instead, they were found to be highly localized. Knowing these very specific regions enables us to understand how the drugs exert their various effects.

It seemed unlikely that the opiate receptors were there by accident. But man was not created with morphine within him. Could the receptors serve normally to interact with some opiate-like chemical occurring naturally in the body?

In Scotland, John Hughes and Hans Kosterlitz were the first to isolate specific chemicals they named "enkephalins," natural opiate-like neurotransmitters. Numerous laboratories then began to search for these substances. Soon, at Johns Hopkins, Rabi Simantov and I also identified them. Additional research showed the intimate association, in various parts of the brain, between enkephalins and opiate receptor sites. As we anticipated, the opiate receptors are in fact enkephalin receptors.

It seemed reasonable to assume that the body's own opiate-like substances might be less addicting than synthetic opiate drugs. Many companies have duplicated enkephalins, and are testing them. Already there are indications that certain of these derivatives may be less addicting than morphine, yet offer significant relief of pain.

The opiate-receptor technology has been extended to demonstrations of receptors for other neurotransmitters. These studies have clarified the actions of many drugs of importance in medicine, including a group relevant to schizophrenia and all the major antianxiety drug agents, such as Librium and Valium.

These recent developments in brain research are just beginning to be applied to studies of specific diseases. One of the most dramatic breakthroughs has to do with Alzheimer's disease, a form of the mental deterioration called dementia.

We have long known that as people age, memory begins to be impaired. When I was a medical student it was generally assumed that this involved some vague loss of neurons because of arteriosclerosis, or hardening of the arteries, in the brain. In some instances this is true. But in the last decade, scientists have learned that in many cases senile dementia is due to the very specific process of Alzheimer's disease.

In 1907 an inquisitive German psychiatrist, *(Continued on page 188)*

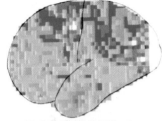

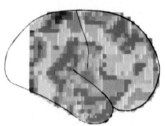

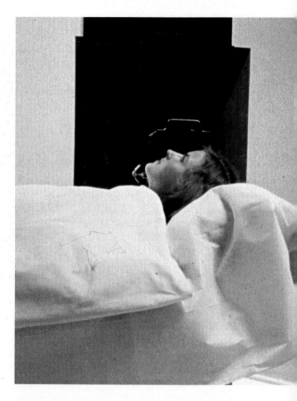

## MAPPING THE BRAIN'S RESPONSES

*Color-coded maps of the cerebral cortex locate specific areas involved in physical and mental activities. At right, images of a woman's brain light up a computer screen in Copenhagen's Bispebjerg Hospital. Above, blood-flow scans using radioactive xenon measure activity levels: blue, reduced flow; green, unchanged; red and orange, higher flows indicating increased activity. (1) and (2) Counting aloud activates areas for mouth-tongue movement and hearing. (3) The resting state shows an active frontal lobe, primary region of planning and reflection. (4) Watching an object lights up centers related to vision and eye movement. (5) Listening stimulates centers for hearing and understanding speech. Below, PET scans locate parts of the brain associated with language and music. (1) In the resting state, the red spot at the back of the brain shows the subject has eyes open. (2) Language animates the hearing center in the left*

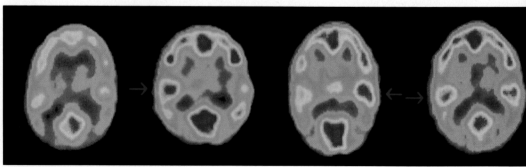

4: LOOKING AT A MOVING OBJECT, LEFT HEMISPHERE

5: LISTENING TO WORDS, LEFT HEMISPHERE

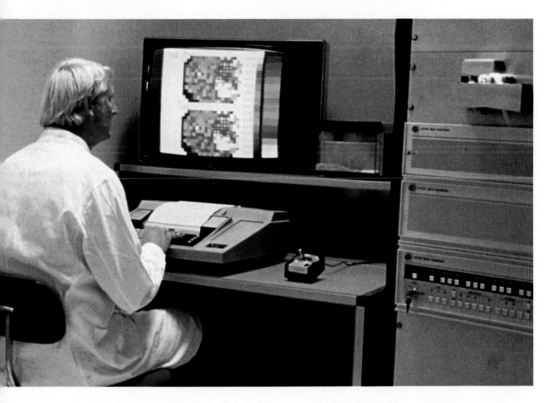

*hemisphere. (3) Listening to music activates the hearing center on the right. (4) Language and music together light up both sides. (5) A musically untrained person listens to differences between two tonal sequences, mentally humming the notes; the right hemisphere shows the major response. (6) A musically trained person uses the left hemisphere to analyze a tonal sequence, visualizing notes on a scale. (7) Even the trained musician falls back on the subjective, nonanalytical right hemisphere when comparing chords.*

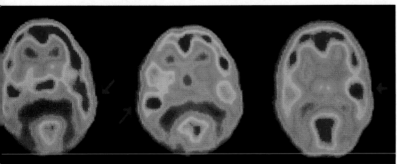

ONAL SEQUENCE, UNTRAINED LISTENER    6: TONAL SEQUENCE, TRAINED LISTENER    7: TONAL QUALITY (CHORDS)

# MESSAGE
# TO A
# SINGLE
# CELL

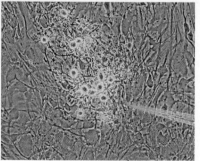

*Using an array of precision equipment, Salk Institute researcher Donna Gruol prepares to place a very small quantity of a neurotransmitter onto a single brain cell. The chemical rests in a specialized pipette, a five-chambered glass tube whose point tapers to microscopic size. At far left, the pipette lies positioned next to a selected neuron (viewed at near left through the microscope). An electrical impulse pushes the chemical particles out of the tube onto the nerve cell, mimicking a neuron's natural way of communicating with other cells. A pipette can also detect electrical signals produced by a neuron, enabling scientists to study its responses to neurotransmitters, as well as to medicines and other drugs.*

Like stars twinkling in the Milky Way, opiate receptors spangle a section of rat spinal cord (right) and rat brain (below). In this sensitive imaging process, developed at the National Institute of Mental Health, a solution containing radioactive morphine bathes the tissues. The receptors take up the opiate, producing whitish spots and streaks that enable researchers to identify the areas of concentration. Normally these receptor sites respond to neurotransmitters called enkephalins, internally produced chemicals that have a molecular shape similar to that of morphine, heroin, and codeine. Like

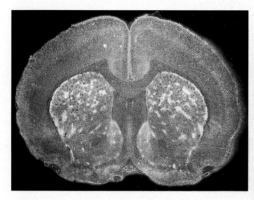

**IDENTIFYING THE OPIATE RECEPTOR SITES**

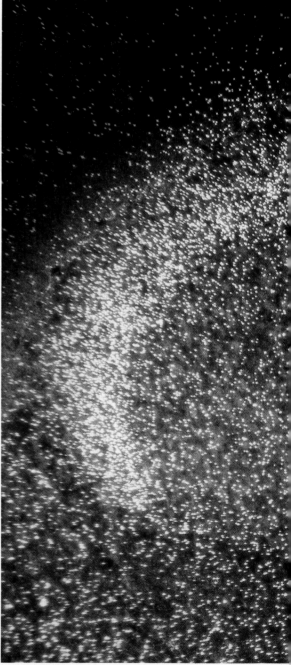

*those opiate drugs, enkephalins can reduce pain by limiting the passage of signals between neurons. When triggered by extreme stress or trauma and bound to receptors in the spinal cord and brain, they block many of the pain messages before they reach the level of conscious awareness.*

Alois Alzheimer, described a profound type of dementia which began at about age 50, and which he therefore referred to as presenile dementia. In his patients Alzheimer found a unique type of deposit and fibrous tangles in the cerebral cortex. For many years after that, it was thought that this type of dementia was extremely rare. Now it is known that most cases of dementia that occur with senility involve the same sorts of changes in the brain. What Dr. Alzheimer had detected were the most severe and thus relatively rare forms, in which the onset occurred at a particularly early age.

Recent research has measured levels of different neurotransmitters in the brains of patients who died with Alzheimer's disease. Most of the transmitters and the enzymes that form them are quite normal. But the enzyme that synthesizes acetylcholine is found to have decreased by as much as 90 percent. Thus there must be a degeneration of acetylcholine-containing neurons in this condition.

Although acetylcholine is one of the most common neurotransmitters, the exact location of the acetylcholine-containing neurons in the brain was not clarified until very recently. Joseph Coyle at Johns Hopkins, among others, demonstrated that the cell bodies of those neurons do not occur within the cerebral cortex itself but in a formation called the basal nucleus. The axons of these cells ascend from the basal nucleus to penetrate into the cerebral cortex.

Discovery of the major acetylcholine pathway to the cerebral cortex certainly suggested that this might be involved in Alzheimer's disease. When Peter Whitehouse, Arthur Clark, and Donald Price examined the brains of patients with Alzheimer's disease, they discovered that there was indeed a loss of neurons of the basal nucleus.

To ensure that their original observations were valid, a controlled study was set up involving 22 brains—11 from people who had had Alzheimer's disease when they died, 11 from individuals of the same age who had shown no symptoms of the disease. Although his associates knew the diagnoses, Dr. Price did not; nevertheless he batted 1.000 in identifying the two groups, because the patients with Alzheimer's disease showed a consistent and selective reduction in nerve cells in the basal nucleus. Thus, loss of one neurotransmitter-specific pathway seems to be a major contributor to the intellectual defects that occur with this malady.

If, as it would appear, Alzheimer's disease is in fact caused by a deficiency of acetylcholine, we should be able to treat its symptoms by prescribing drugs that mimic that particular chemical transmitter. Experimental studies are under way with such medications.

Most of the new developments in brain research have been made possible by novel techniques. Many of these are biochemical and involve the use of radioactive substances. Some of the most relevant techniques have to do with monitoring the brain activities of living persons.

Until recently it has not been possible to detect subtle abnormalities in brain structure. Conventional X rays reveal only the bony skull. A recent modification of X-ray technology called "computerized tomography," or CT, has permitted direct, detailed visualization of the structures of the brain and most of the soft-tissue organs of the body.

The CT scanner shows abnormalities in structure, but not in function. In many diseases one might expect that alterations in function would precede deterioration of the organ itself by a considerable period of time. "Positron emission tomography," or PET scanning, extends the principles of tomographic or "cross-section" scanning to an evaluation of the functioning of various parts of the body. In 1974, Michael Phelps and his colleagues at Washington University in St. Louis developed the PET scanner to monitor the activity of neurons in specific parts of the brain. The technique involves injecting the subject with a short-lived radioactive solution. The PET camera, like the CT scanner, looks at the brain from many angles; but in this instance, instead of aiming X rays *at* the brain, the camera detects the emission of radioactive particles *from* the brain.

The possibilities for application of the PET scanner are far reaching. Are opiate receptors abnormal in heroin

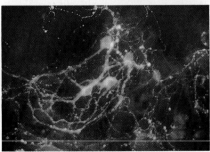

addicts? Are there changes in certain receptors in schizophrenics? These questions, as well as many others, can now be addressed.

What lies ahead in brain research? Of course, no one knows for certain. Indeed, what makes the field so exciting is that surprises happen every day.

Still, let me try a few educated guesses. The pace of basic discoveries about brain functioning has been escalating. We are beginning to understand fundamental mechanisms so clearly that we can now apply our knowledge more and more reliably to human subjects. The PET scanner and an even newer diagnostic system, NMR (for "nuclear magnetic resonance"), are among the tools that may help us bridge the gap between the laboratory and the clinic.

In the next decade, I suspect that we will be able to observe in living humans receptors for all the known neurotransmitters and drugs. We will probably be able to measure the activity of neurons throughout the brain in awake, actively thinking and feeling humans.

Such techniques ought to give us at least a fighting chance of detecting specific abnormalities related to the major mental disorders. Perhaps we will find what is selectively aberrant in the biochemical functioning of a schizophrenic's brain. Perhaps we will find clues to the reasons for the remarkable mood swings of manic depressive patients.

My highest hopes are for development of more selective drugs. As we refine these and increase our understanding of neurotransmitter receptors, it may be possible to use doses so low that the drugs will not produce unwanted side effects. Indeed, we may be able to tailor drugs to produce extremely subtle and precise changes in states of feeling and conceptualizing.

I anticipate that the delicate modulation of mental functions with drugs will contribute greatly to alleviating all forms of emotional disorder. I predict better therapies for conditions ranging from the most severe psychoses to everyday "blues" and neurotic anxiety. Surely relieving mental and emotional distress in a large proportion of mankind has positive implications for the future of an ever more complex society.

# THE TOLL OF DEMENTIA

Senile dementia erodes the mental faculties of about 15 percent of the elderly. At right, neurons sprout multiple branchings until adulthood. With age, some cells show degenerative changes; with senile dementia, losses increase greatly. CT and PET scans display butterfly-shaped ventricles— spaces filled with spinal fluid—that have enlarged to compensate for atrophy of brain tissue. The PET scan's predominance of blues and greens indicates reduced activity, typical of dementia. Also typical: reduced flow of blood, as seen in the xenon scans; blue represents low blood flow. Below, the microscope discloses structural changes in Alzheimer's disease, a dementia that may strike before old age: (1) neurons in normal numbers; (2) loss of neurons that contain acetylcholine, a neurotransmitter used in learning and memory; (3) tangles, twisted filaments inside pyramidal brain cells; (4) neuritic plaques, deposits of enlarged nerve terminals around abnormal protein.

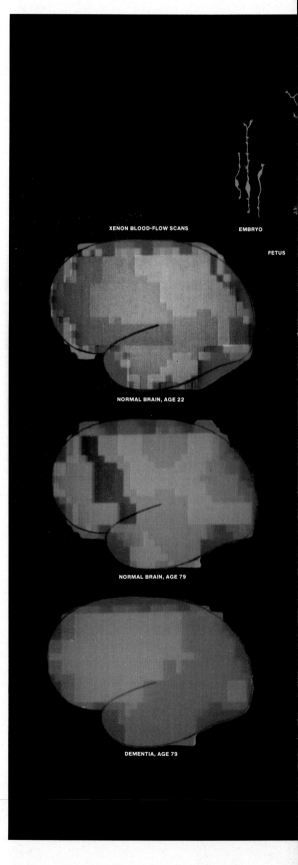

XENON BLOOD-FLOW SCANS

EMBRYO

FETUS

NORMAL BRAIN, AGE 22

NORMAL BRAIN, AGE 79

DEMENTIA, AGE 79

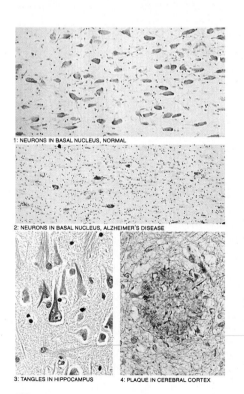

1: NEURONS IN BASAL NUCLEUS, NORMAL

2: NEURONS IN BASAL NUCLEUS, ALZHEIMER'S DISEASE

3: TANGLES IN HIPPOCAMPUS

4: PLAQUE IN CEREBRAL CORTEX

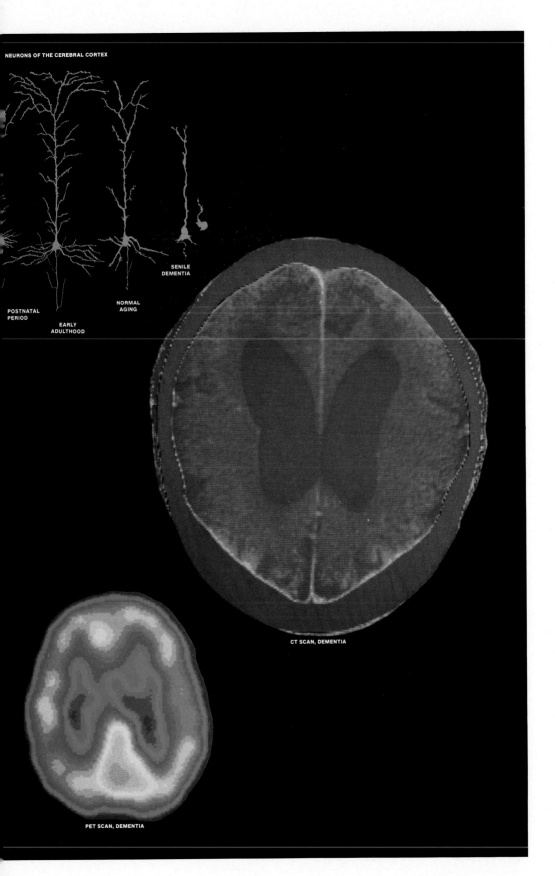

NEURONS OF THE CEREBRAL CORTEX

POSTNATAL
PERIOD

EARLY
ADULTHOOD

NORMAL
AGING

SENILE
DEMENTIA

CT SCAN, DEMENTIA

PET SCAN, DEMENTIA

## LANGUAGE AND
## THE ORGANIZATION
## OF THE BRAIN

*Incandescent bulbs attached to a man's arm and hand create swirling patterns of light during Salk Institute studies of how the brain processes sign language. James Tucker, born deaf, signals a phrase; a television monitor on the floor repeats his motions. Below at right, while researcher Greg Chesney watches sign language on a video screen, electrodes record his mental activity in* *the form of brain waves. Opposite, his eyeglass lens captures a reflection of the screen. In this double exposure, wave patterns in color follow the rhythm of his brain's electrical activity. By comparing brain-wave responses of those who can hear with those born deaf, scientists hope to determine the effect of early language experience on the functional organization of the brain.*

*Antibody:* one of the millions of proteins made by certain cells of the immune system. The major function of antibodies is to defend against disease.

*Antigen:* substance that stimulates the immune system to produce an antibody. For example, an antigen could be a toxin or a "recognition site" molecule on the surface of an invading bacterium.

*Black hole:* volume of space containing an extremely compact concentration of matter resulting from the collapse of a massive star. The gravitational force of the black hole is so great that not even light can escape.

*Brain stem:* portion of the brain that connects with the spinal cord. The brain stem is responsible for many basic functions of the body.

*Cardiovascular system:* network of arteries, veins, and the heart that circulates oxygen to tissues and carries away carbon dioxide.

*Cerebellum:* portion of the brain beneath the cerebrum, associated with coordinating voluntary movement.

*Cerebral cortex:* mantle covering the cerebrum's two hemispheres. The cortex is associated with speech, thought, memory, and imagination.

*Cerebrum:* largest part of the brain, composed of the twin cerebral hemispheres and smaller sections that integrate the brain's major activities.

*Cloning:* asexual reproduction of a cell or organism to create a group of genetically identical individuals.

*Continental drift:* concept that the continents slowly move about, riding on huge plates or sections of the earth's shell.

*Corona:* outermost part of the solar atmosphere, consisting of extremely hot, thin gas.

*Cosmic ray:* stream of highly energetic nuclei that bombard the earth's atmosphere from space. Cosmic rays collide with atoms in the atmosphere and produce nuclear particles.

*DNA:* deoxyribonucleic acid, the genetic material contained in every cell. It is composed of nucleotides and arranged in a double helix structure.

*Dementia:* mental deterioration resulting from degeneration of nerve cells in the brain, caused by any of various diseases.

*Dendroclimatology:* science that deals with the correlation of the growth rings of tree trunks with climatic conditions.

*Elementary particle:* one of the fundamental, indivisible bits of matter. Leptons and quarks are now generally considered to be those basic constituents. Some scientists include the photon, the basic unit of light, as an elementary particle.

*Enkephalin:* naturally produced opiate-like neurotransmitter.

*Eucaryote:* organism whose cell or cells contain a nucleus.

*Fault:* fracture in the earth's shell. On either side of the fracture the earth moves or has moved relative to the other side.

*Genetic engineering:* modifying an organism's DNA for a specific purpose; for example, to produce a useful natural substance not easily synthesized in the laboratory.

*Hot spot:* localized area of heat rising from the earth's interior. Its presence is inferred from volcanic activity.

*Hybridoma:* hybrid cell resulting from the fusing of a cancer cell with another cell. Hybridomas can be made to produce large quantities of a specific antibody.

*Hypothalamus:* portion of the brain that initiates hormone release from the pituitary gland—thus linking the nervous

system to the endocrine, or hormonal, system.

*Immune system:* natural defense mechanism of the body that resists infectious agents. Its chief functional elements are lymphocytes and other white blood cells.

*Insulin:* protein important in utilizing glucose in the blood.

*Interferon:* protein made in minute quantities by cells to help combat viral invasion.

*Isotope:* variant form of a chemical element.

*Lava:* molten rock that has reached the earth's surface.

*Lepton:* one of a class of elementary particles. Among the leptons are the electron, with its negative charge, and the neutrino, which has no charge.

*Lithosphere:* rigid outer layer or shell of the earth. The lithosphere is broken into a number of slowly moving plates.

*Magma:* molten rock beneath the earth's surface.

*Mantle:* semi-rigid interior layer of the earth. The top part of the mantle is considered to be part of the lithosphere.

*Mid-Atlantic Ridge:* volcanic mountain range along the middle of the Atlantic Ocean. Zone of seafloor spreading; part of the Mid-Ocean Ridge.

*Mid-Ocean Ridge:* ridge traversing the oceans of the earth. Zone of seafloor spreading.

*Neuron:* cell of the nervous system. Made up of a cell body and its extensions—numerous dendrites and, usually, one axon—it helps carry out the body's internal communications and control.

*Neurotransmitter:* chemical, released by neurons, that affects the activity of neighboring nerves or muscles.

*Nuclear transplantation:* method used to clone organisms. Nuclei from one organism (usually an embryo) are substituted for the nuclei of eggs of the same species. The new individuals are identical.

*Nucleosynthesis:* process of nuclear reactions within a star or supernova resulting in the conversion of hydrogen into other chemical elements.

*Nucleotide:* component molecule of DNA. The sequence of nucleotides along the DNA chain determines heredity and protein manufacture. In DNA, each nucleotide is composed of a sugar-phosphate group and a nitrogenous base (adenine, guanine, cytosine, or thymine).

*Organelle:* one of the internal structures of a cell. The largest is the nucleus.

*Photon:* smallest unit of light or other radiant energy.

*Pituitary:* gland at the base of the brain, controlled by the hypothalamus, that secretes hormones to regulate bodily functions.

*Plasmid:* closed loop of bacterial DNA, often used in genetic engineering.

*Plate tectonics:* theory proposing that the earth's shell is made up of rigid plates that move about, resulting in continental drift, earthquakes, and volcanic activity.

*Procaryote:* simple, single-celled organism without a nucleus, such as a bacterium.

*Quark:* one of the elementary particles of which all other particles except leptons and photons are believed to be formed.

*Quasar:* quasi-stellar object. Mysterious, very distant starlike source of radio and optical signals that seems to emit more energy than a hundred galaxies.

*Radiometric dating:* technique to determine the age of rocks and other geological material by measuring the relative amounts of radioactive elements they contain.

*Red shift:* displacement of the spectral pattern of an astronomical body toward the longer, or red,

CLOUDS OF PINK IONIZED GAS AND COSMIC DUST FLOAT IN THE DIRECTION OF THE CENTER OF OUR GALAXY, BEYOND THE CONSTELLATION SAGITTARIUS.

wavelengths—usually because the source is moving away from the observer.

*Relativity:* concept of Albert Einstein that is used as a basis for theoretical models of the universe. His Special Theory, published in 1905, holds that motion, time, and distance are not absolute but relative to moving frames of reference. His second or General Theory, published in 1916, extends the Special Theory to include acceleration and gravitation.

*Restriction enzyme:* one of more than 350 bacterial proteins apparently developed as protection against invading viruses. Such an enzyme cuts DNA at a specific point in a nucleotide sequence. Restriction enzymes are used in genetic research and engineering.

*Rift valley:* valley along a zone of tectonic tension—often under the ocean at the Mid-Ocean Ridge, but also occurring on the land surface, as in East Africa.

*Seafloor spreading:* moving apart of the earth's plates in ridge zones under the sea. Magma wells up from the earth's mantle, forming new crustal material.

*Seismic gap:* zone where two plates meet but where tectonic tension has not been released over a long period of time. Such areas are likely locations of future earthquakes.

*Seismology:* science concerned with movements of the earth, primarily earthquakes.

*Supernova:* gigantic stellar explosion in which the star's luminosity suddenly increases by a vast amount. Most of the star's substance is blown away, leaving behind an expanding shell of gas (the supernova remnant) and a very dense core (sometimes a black hole).

## Additional Reading

The reader may want to check the *National Geographic Index* for related articles and to refer to the following books. SCIENTISTS AND THEIR TOOLS: Adriano Buzzati-Traverso, *The Scientific Enterprise, Today and Tomorrow;* Horace Freeland Judson, *The Search for Solutions;* Derek deSolla Price, *Science Since Babylon.* THE UNIVERSE: QUASARS TO QUARKS: Eric Chaisson, *Cosmic Dawn;* Herbert Friedman, *The Amazing Universe;* Lloyd Motz, *The Universe;* Paul Murdin and David Allen, *The Catalogue of the Universe;* James S. Trefil, *From Atoms to Quarks;* Steven Weinberg, *The First Three Minutes: A Modern View of the Origin of the Universe.* THE FAMILY OF THE SUN: J. Kelly Beatty, Brian O'Leary, and Andrew Chaikin, editors, *The New Solar System;* Joseph H. Jackson and John H. Baumert, *Pictorial Guide to the Planets;* Bruce Murray, Michael C. Malin, and Ronald Greeley, *Earthlike Planets; Fire of Life: The Smithsonian Book of the Sun.* OUR CHANGING PLANET EARTH: John Imbrie and Katherine Palmer Imbrie, *Ice Ages: Solving the Mystery;* Frank Press and Raymond Siever, *Earth;* Walter Sullivan, *Continents in Motion.* PROBING THE NEW BIOLOGY: S. E. Luria, *Life: the Unfinished Experiment;* Lynn Margulis and Karlene V. Schwartz, *Five Kingdoms;* James D. Watson, *The Double Helix* and *Molecular Biology of the Gene.* ADVANCES IN MEDICAL RESEARCH: June Goodfield, *The Siege of Cancer;* Zsolt Harsanyi and Richard Hutton, *Genetic Prophecy: Beyond the Double Helix;* E. Brad Thompson, *Cancer: What is It?* (National Institutes of Health pamphlet). WONDERS OF THE BRAIN: Donald B. Calne, *The Brain* (NIH pamphlet); John C. Eccles, *The Understanding of the Brain;* Scientific American, *The Brain.*

## Notes on Contributors

DEREK DESOLLA PRICE taught science and mathematics in England and Singapore before coming to the United States. He has been writing and lecturing on science history at Yale since 1960. Dr. Price was the first president of the International Council for Science Policy Studies. In 1976 he received the Leonardo da Vinci Medal, the major award of the Society for the History of Technology.

Combining nuclear physics with astronomy and geochemistry, DONALD D. CLAYTON pursues an active schedule of teaching and research in Texas for most of each year, and in Europe—usually at Cambridge or Heidelberg—in the summer. A graduate of Southern Methodist and Caltech, he is the author of a widely used textbook on stellar evolution.

BRADFORD A. SMITH, a member of the University of Arizona's distinguished space sciences faculty, began his scientific career as a chemical engineer but soon concentrated on his interest in astronomy. In addition to his teaching responsibilities at Arizona, he is leader of the imaging team for the Voyager space-exploration program.

Over a span of 31 years as professor of geophysics at the University of Toronto, J. TUZO WILSON made numerous major contributions to our growing understanding of this planet. Winner of the Vetlesen Prize in Earth Sciences in 1978, he became soon thereafter the president of the American Geophysical Union. At present he directs the highly popular Ontario Science Centre in Toronto.

RICHARD F. THOMPSON's area of research concerns the mechanisms of learning and memory and combines the disciplines of psychology, biology, and neurology. Formerly at Oregon, Harvard, and UC-Irvine, he is now chairman of the Human Biology Program at Stanford. To graduate student Richard C. Cassin, Dr. Thompson extends thanks for invaluable assistance in the preparation of the chapter "Probing the New Biology."

ANTHONY CERAMI is head of the Laboratory of Medical Biochemistry at Rockefeller University. His team of investigators seeks better understanding and more effective treatment of disease. In 1978 Dr. Cerami received the David Rumbough Scientific Award for diabetes research.

Ever since SOLOMON H. SNYDER joined the medical faculty of Johns Hopkins University in 1966, he has been intensively engaged in studying the relationships of mental functions and the body's chemical substances. Now director of the Department of Neuroscience, he has won numerous prizes for scientific achievement, including the Albert Lasker Medical Research Award in 1978.

A former news photographer, MARK GODFREY spent four years in the Far East. More recently he has specialized in the photographic interpretation of scientific subjects. For National Geographic's Special Publications Division he has previously photographed *The Mighty Aztecs* and contributed to *Exploring America's Backcountry.*

SUSAN SANFORD, the National Geographic staff artist who created the paintings for this book, holds a master of science degree in medical and biological illustration from the University of Michigan. The versatile Ms. Sanford is also a sculptor, scrimshaw artist, and bookbinder.

## Acknowledgments

The Special Publications Division is grateful to the individuals and organizations named or quoted in the text and to those cited here for their generous cooperation and assistance during the preparation of this book: French Anderson, Diana Araujo, Silvio A. Bedini, Dennis Blakeslee, Geoffrey A. Briggs, Louis L. Bucciarelli, Richard C. Cassin, Charles L. Drake, Donald S. Fredrickson, William Friedewald, Dennis Goode, Karen Greendale, Theodore R. Gull, Alan D. Hecht, Michael Kotewicz, Richard Matzner, Norman Metzger, George W. Moore, National Aeronautics and Space Administration, National Institutes of Health, Mike Ross, LeRoy N. Sanchez, Peter B. Stifel, E. Brad Thompson, James S. Trefil, Timothy Triche, U. S. Geological Survey, Jurrie Van der Woude, Voyager Science Teams, Robert F. Weaver, Julius Weber.

**PHOTOGRAPHIC CREDITS**

S. Christian Simonson, III, University of Maryland/Jody Bolt, N.G.S. Staff (hardcover); Robert Langridge, UCSF Computer Graphics Laboratory (1); © 1977 Anglo-Australian Telescope Board/David Malin (2-3); Manfred Kage/ PETER ARNOLD, INC. (5).

**SCIENTISTS AND THEIR TOOLS:** Fred Ward/BLACK STAR (8 upper); Robert W. Decker (9 upper); Valerie Paul (8-9 center); Chris Springmann/BLACK STAR (9 center); Steve Northup/BLACK STAR (9 center right); Mark Godfrey (8 lower left, 9 lower left, 24 upper left); J. M. Hayes (9 lower right); Lawrence Livermore National Laboratory (10 upper); Douglas Kirkland/CONTACT (10 center & lower, 11); Los Alamos National Laboratory (12-13); Gary Ladd (14-15); Naval Research Laboratory (17); NASA (19); N.G.S. Photographer Steve Raymer (20-21); Rick Hoblitt, USGS (21 upper); Brian R. Wolff (22 upper); Dr. R. A. Robb, Mayo Clinic (22 lower); © 1982 Howard Sochurek (24 upper right, 25 left); Dan McCoy/BLACK STAR (24 lower left, 27 right all); Dan McCoy/RAINBOW (24 lower right, 25 lower right, 26-27); Fonar Corporation/SCIENCE PHOTO LIBRARY (25 upper & center right).

**THE UNIVERSE: QUASARS TO QUARKS:** © 1981 Anglo-Australian Telescope Board/David Malin (28-29, 40-41); © 1979 AATB/David Malin (42-43); H. F. Dylla, Princeton Plasma Physics Laboratory (30-31); Mark Godfrey (33, 34 left, center, lower, 35, 54, 58-59, 63, 64-65); U. S. Department of Energy (34 right); © 1965 California Institute of Technology (36 upper); Jean L. Lorre, Jet Propulsion Laboratory and Mt. Wilson Observatory (36-37 center, 37 upper & lower); Herman J. Kokojan (39); © 1979 Royal Observatory, Edinburgh/David Malin (44-45); Kerby Smith and Brick Price (47); © Ira Wyman (49 upper); NASA (49 lower); Douglas W. Johnson, Battelle Observatory (50-51); National Radio Astronomy Observatory (51 upper & right); Homer Sykes/WOODFIN CAMP (52 upper, 53); Lick Observatory (52 lower left); Jean L. Lorre/SCIENCE PHOTO LIBRARY (52 lower right); Mickey Pfleger (61); Dan McCoy/RAINBOW (62 upper); James F. Quinn (62 left).

**THE FAMILY OF THE SUN:** Big Bear Solar Observatory, C.I.T. (66-67); High Altitude Observatory, National Center for Atmospheric Research (68 left); Dan McCoy/RAINBOW (68-69); Mark Godfrey (74 upper, 84 lower, 90-91); Bartholomew Nagy (74 lower); NASA (76-77, 79 left, 80, 81 lower left, upper right, 82-83); Tass from SOVFOTO (78-79); JPL/NASA (79 right, 81 upper left, lower right, 85, 87-89); Douglas Kirkland/CONTACT (84 upper); composite photo by W. M. Sinton, University of Hawaii (91 upper); University of Arizona (91 center); U. S. Naval Observatory (91 lower).

**OUR CHANGING PLANET EARTH:** Rick Hoblitt, USGS (92-93); N.G.S. Photographer Emory Kristof and Alvin M. Chandler, N.G.S. Staff, by remote-control camera (94-95); John Edmond/M.I.T. and National Science Foundation (95 upper); Woods Hole Oceanographic Institution (95 center); N.G.S. Photographer Emory Kristof (95 lower); Dr. Rick Grigg (98-99); NASA (100-101); Georg Gerster (102-103, 104 lower, 105 lower & right, 111 right, 116); Loren McIntyre (104-105); John Bryson/SYGMA (107); Stern/BLACK STAR (110); Mark Godfrey (111 left both); Dan Dzurisin, USGS (112-113 upper); Terry Leighley, USGS (113 upper); N.G.S. Photographer Steve Raymer (112-113 lower, 113 right); John C. Lahr, USGS (114 upper); George Plafker, USGS (114 lower); Craig P. Berg (114-115); Steve Earley (118-119); Jim Brandenburg (120); Peter J. Axelson, University of New Hampshire (122-123).

**PROBING THE NEW BIOLOGY:** Robert Langridge, UCSF/RAINBOW (124-125); J. M. Hayes (128-129); UCLA (129 upper); J. William Schopf (129 center); Elso S. Barghoorn (129 lower); George Watchmaker, Lawrence Livermore National Laboratory (132-133, 135 upper); Harry Howard (135 lower); Mark Godfrey (136-137, 140-143, 146); Louise T. Chow, Carter Burwell, and Thomas R. Broker, Cold Spring Harbor Laboratory (138 upper); Dr. Jack Griffith (138 lower); Steve Northup/BLACK STAR (147).

**ADVANCES IN MEDICAL SCIENCE:** James Balog/BLACK STAR (148-150); Mark Godfrey (151, 158-159 lower both); Dr. Andrejs Liepins/SCIENCE PHOTO LIBRARY (152-153); Prof. A. R. Lawton/SCIENCE PHOTO LIBRARY (157); © 1980 David Scharf (158 upper both); Margaret R. Abernathy, M.D., Division of Thermography, Georgetown University Medical Center (160 lower both); N.G.S. Photographer James L. Stanfield (160-161); Eastern Virginia Medical School (162 upper & center); Bob Strong/BLACK STAR (162 lower); Nathan Benn (164-165); Dr. William Annesley, Wills Eye Hospital, Retina Service (165 right all); Brian Payne (166-167); Dan McCoy/BLACK STAR (169); Dan McCoy/RAINBOW (170 upper); Bill Pierce/RAINBOW (170 lower); Steve Northup/BLACK STAR (171).

**WONDERS OF THE BRAIN:** Robert B. Livingston, M.D., UCSD (172-173); Mark Godfrey (174-175, 184-185, 189 upper, 192-193); Dr. Julius Weber (177); Anne B. K. Krumbhaar, N.G.S. Staff (180); Niels A. Lassen, M.D./Copenhagen (182-183 upper & center); courtesy of Dr. Michael E. Phelps and Dr. John C. Mazziotta, UCLA School of Medicine, photos by Dan McCoy/RAINBOW (182-183 lower); Miles Herkenham/RAINBOW, from work of Miles Herkenham and Candace Pert (186-187); George Uhl, Joseph Neale, Jeffrey Barker, and Solomon H. Snyder (189 lower); Donald L. Price (190 left all); Georg Deutsch (190 right all); Arnold B. Scheibel, M.D., Brain Research Institute, UCLA Medical Center (190-191 upper); Dan McCoy/RAINBOW (191 right); Brookhaven National Laboratory and New York University Medical Center (191 lower).

© 1981 Anglo-Australian Telescope Board/David Malin (195).

# INDEX

**Library of Congress CIP Data:**

Main entry under title:
Frontiers of science.
    Bibliography: p.
    Includes index.
    Contents: Scientists and their tools / by Derek deSolla Price—The universe—quasars to quarks / by Donald D. Clayton—The family of the sun / by Bradford A. Smith—[etc.]
    1. Science—Addresses, essays, lectures.
I. Price, Derek deSolla.    II. National Geographic Society (U. S.). Special Publications Division.   III. Title: On the brink of tomorrow.
Q171.F89 1982     500     82-18978
ISBN 0-87044-414-X
ISBN 0-87044-419-O (lib. bdg.)

Composition for *Frontiers of Science* by National Geographic's Photographic Services, Carl M. Shrader, Director, Lawrence F. Ludwig, Assistant Director. Printed and bound by Holladay-Tyler Printing Corp., Rockville, Md. Color separations by the Lanman Progressive Co., Washington, D. C., and N.E.C., Inc., Nashville, Tenn.